When a Dragon Winks

Emmett Eiland

Published by
Emmett Eiland, Inc.
emmetteilandinc@gmail.com

Copyright
© 2009 Emmett Eiland

ISBN
ISBN-10 - 1442127929

Production
Book production by Dave Brown Design,
dave@davebrowndesign.com
Cover by Nik Eakle Graphics,
nikeakle@gmail.com

Prologue

The first mention and still the best discussion of the Ferrier Dragon Rug appeared in *A History of Oriental Carpets Before 1800*, written by F. R. Martin and published in 1908. Seeking to understand the history of Oriental rugs, Martin had researched, among other things, every travel book from the time of the Greek Empire to the beginning of the 19th century, searching for mention of what we now call Oriental rugs. One of his important discoveries had been *Travels in Disguise*, written in 1692 by the Frenchman, L. B. Ferrier, about his travels in Turkey, Iran, Turkmenistan, Samarkand and China. As translated by Martin himself, the Ferrier passage that has since intrigued so many rug scholars and collectors is as follows:

"Having entered China dressed and, I hoped, sufficiently disguised as a Chinese monk, and having established myself (by means of signs I made with my hands) as a holy man who had taken vows of silence, I was permitted to go wherever I wished—that is, I dare say, where no European had ever trod before. I was forever in fear of being discovered, and in morbid moments I wondered whether, if I were unveiled as a fraud, my punishment might be to have my tongue cut out so that I might truly be what I seemed, a mute.

It seemed to me that, as a holy man, my status was ambiguous to the guardians of gates, so to speak, They did not know what to do with me and simply left me alone to do whatever I would. So it was that, after just a few gestures with my hands, I was able to enter unhindered the fabulous palace of Ling Sui Wen with my filthy feet and the few rags I wore. I was left alone to sleep in whatever corner I could find, as long as I was not too much in the way of the kitchen workers or others who had duties.

So it was that I left my corner of a hallway one night and went in search of what I had heard rumors of, the "inner Palace." Guided by the word "inner," which I took quite literally to refer to the interior or central part of the palace, I wound through the hallways always choosing the central-most way, striving always to reach the heart of the palace or its innermost geography. Of course no sign marked such a territory, nor could I have read it if one had. No, there was no sign at all and no guard nor barrier nor dragon but for the one I shall presently describe. But presently I was convinced I had gained the inner palace. I was so informed by the simplicity and dignity of all I saw, just as one divines the difference between an office of commerce and a church. This seemed to me to be a cathedral, a place of worship, an area, as it were, of spirit. Guttering candles lit the room and led me to its center, and there lay a rug made of wool pile, and nothing lay on it but its own design. On the rug's saffron yellow ground lay a dragon, or, rather, there floated or flew a dragon, his head not directly in the rug's center but somewhat to one side, and he seemed to look into my eyes. He was wingless, four-legged, fanged and clawed— bristling, blue, bescaled, magnificent— a five-toed dragon royal. Never, before that moment, had I been anything other than amused by the dragons in Chinese carpets. They had struck me as comically fierce, mere cartoons. But in that light, or in that chamber, or perhaps because of the danger I was in of being discovered, my dragon thrilled me through. But, really, it was none of that, the strange light or the danger I was in, it was his eyes. "Who are you?" they seemed to ask.

"Why have you wandered from your homeland and your people? Why do you disguise yourself among strangers? What do you hide?"

Though soon I retreated from the chamber, I was haunted [*envoutant* in Ferrier's original French text] and am haunted still by the dragon's eyes glaring into mine, asking questions for which I had no answers."

That is the passage that Martin translated at the beginning of the 20th century and which, for more than a hundred years since then, has caused so much speculation, confrontation and refutation among rug scholars and collectors. Martin adds his own speculation as follows.

"First, did the rug exist at all or did Ferrier create it from whole cloth? Did he really wander China posed as a mute monk, and if he did, did his disguise really give him access to the inner sanctum he describes? Then, as now, a good story sells travel books.

"And yet his description of the dragon rug rings true: its saffron field, the fearsome blue dragon with scales and five toes. Why was it woven? Who commissioned it? If ever it surfaces we will be able to analyze the details of its construction and will finally unlock its mysteries.

"We do know that later in his narrative Ferrier casts off his disguise and vows never again to "seem to be what I am not, for I had been haunted by the dragon's eyes," he says, "which seemed to ask why I did not join the ranks of honest people. No longer would I seek to gain their trust by currying sympathy or fear. I would be myself and travel as what I was, a French adventurer in fabulous lands seeking impressions for a book, a man whose life had been changed by the eyes of a dragon." And, according to his account, Ferrier, who had traveled the world essentially as a con artist living off the deluded good will of his hosts, was as good as his word and never again traveled in disguise.

"But, again, what of the Ferrier dragon rug? If it was real, will we ever find it? And will we recognize the rug by the dragon's eyes? Surely, of all the rugs that may never have existed, this must be the most fascinating."

Chapter One

"Lock 'Em Up!"

 Holden stood peering down the laundry chute he called "the black hole of Calcutta." He squinted into its darkness and then sniffed the air, hoping that his rugs and bags and tent bands were still down there, safe from moths and rodents and moisture. Sniffing told him that the last moth crystals he had thrown in had lost their pep. Anxiously, he pulled back from the laundry chute, straightened and snatched a can of "Moth Ice Crystals...no clinging odors" from a shelf beside him. He shook out a palm-full of moth balls and tossed them down the black hole of Calcutta.

Calmed by this ritual, Holden Carter closed the small door of the laundry chute and took a moment to look around before returning to work. He settled cross legged on a mattress that lay directly on the floor without box-springs. The bed was neatly made. From where he sat on it in the gloomy light, he surveyed most of his household possessions: the bed, a couple of colorful small baskets from Shiraz, a nice cherry-wood dresser and, in the kitchen across the hall, a microwave oven and a toaster. Dishes were neatly arranged in a drying-rack beside the sink. He lived in the rear third of an old stucco building on Telegraph Avenue in Berkeley, near Alcatraz Avenue, and, though his apartment was small, it was big enough for a young man who was trying to make his start in life.

Holden was 27, old enough to have all but completed work on a Master's degree in Art History, then to have left the ivory tower, impatient for what he had considered real life: a hands-on life of buying and selling; the life of an art dealer.

He roused himself and left his bedroom. A few feet down the dark hallway, he pushed aside a curtain partition between the front and rear portions of the building and slipped from his living quarters into his showroom. Here the light was brighter and he blinked. A plate glass window passed soft winter sunlight from the street, and spotlights mounted overhead brightened the walls. A passerby on the sidewalk outside would have seen a sign painted above the door: *Holden Carter, Oriental Rugs*.

Restless, he began to prowl the familiar showroom, tracing a path he had stalked countless times before. He sniffed at his hand, the one he had filled with moth crystals a few minutes earlier, then stopped before a rug mounted on a wall, and it seemed to him that it told a story—not the kind of story rug dealers like to tell, not the story of a-maiden-weeping-for-her-lost-lover-and-every-knot-she-ties-in-the-carpet-is-a-tear-of-loneliness—not that kind of story, but a story of where Holden had discovered the rug he now peered at and how he had come to be a rug dealer, and, gradually, how his business had begun to fail.

It was a late 19th century piece that, as far as he knew, was virtually one-of-a-kind. Holden had settled into the belief that it had been woven in the far eastern part of Anatolia, probably by Kurdish weavers, and that it was what some called a "Turkish Kazak" or "Kurdish Kazak." It was coarse and vigorous and boldly colored: geometric, tribal, shaggy, exciting.

Holden remembered how his hands shook when he spied it for sale at the Alameda County Flea Market, only a small corner of it visible. He had invited himself up into the bed of the seller's pickup truck for a closer look. He stared at the small bit of it that was exposed, and something about its colors and the geometry of its design excited him. Then he looked around at the milling flea-market crowd. From his vantage point, standing in the bed of the truck, he could see at least three people converging on the rug, people with the purposeful look of collectors or rug dealers on a hot trail. "How much is it?" he asked the rug's owner, making a preemptive strike.

"Well," the gabby owner started, "I got that rug from a picker in..." One of the people who had been closing in on the rug had reached the pickup and was trying to climb in, his eye on the carpet.

"Just tell me how much!" Holden demanded, rude by necessity.

"Well, I..."

The newcomer asked, too. "How much?" Others were arriving.

"I asked first," Holden said. The owner seemed unable to take the sudden pressure of market demand and was speechless. Holden took the bull by the horns. "I'll give you $200," he said quietly so his competitors could not hear and raise his bid.

"You will?"

"I will! I do! Sold!" Holden shouted, barely in control of himself. His hands shook even more as he opened his wallet and pulled out $200 in tens and fives and ones, aware of the others who were now milling around, staring resentfully at him and at what little they could see of the rug.

"Okay, I guess," the fellow said and took Holden's money. "But is this thing valuable or something?"

"How do I know? I haven't seen it!" And the truth of what he said came crashing down on him. Just a small corner of the rug had he seen. What the hell had he just bought?

He had bought a wonderful rug, powerful and magical. Two years later, it lay mounted before him on the wall of his store, still powerful, magical and still unsold.

Yes, the rug told a story of how he had found it and how he had somehow managed to pay for it and how it had become part of his opening inventory and, finally, of how he had failed to sell it. He hadn't sold it or any of his rugs because no one was buying. End of story.

He had heard of an African tribe that was said to urinate in rituals on objects to make them powerful. In the West, rather than urine, it was *age* that imbued objects with power and value. Nothing made a piece of furniture more desirable than to uncover it in an attic where it had been stashed away for 200 years. Oriental rugs, he believed, owned their mystique—their fabled reputations as magic carpets and flying carpets—to the fact that often they survived long enough to become quite old. The older a rug, the more valued it was. Nevertheless, as Holden's antique rugs grew six months older and then a year and finally two years older while going unsold in his store, rather than gaining in power and value, they began to lose their magic for him. It was hard to stay in love with rugs that had been passed over by so many shoppers.

Finally Holden quit his pacing and, now, sitting at his old roll top desk, gazing at its many little cubbies and shelves and drawers as he had so often before, Holden thought about the rugs and carpets at the bottom of the black hole of Calcutta. Two years ago, a customer had given him an old animal strap—a belt-sized piece woven in Afghanistan, probably made to tie a load to a donkey. It had little commercial value. What should he do with it? He threw it down the old laundry shoot in his bedroom and resolved to do the same in the future with any rug or carpet he got for nothing or next-to-nothing. "Drop it down the hatch and then forget it," he counseled himself. Then, someday, he told himself, he would break into the chute, and there would be his 401K, the only retirement plan he would ever have. After further reflection he refined the plan: He would follow every deposit with a hand-full of moth crystals. And from that time he had made irregular though substantial contributions to the black hole. If a rug was free or cheap, it went down the laundry chute.

Soon he would need to break into it to keep his business alive for one more month.

A customer banged in, bringing a winter chill through the door with him. He stalked the store without glancing at the shop's young proprietor. Customer sightings were generally unfruitful occasions in Holden's experience, and he was slow to awaken from his worries. But the man in his shop was a whirlwind. He spun from one rug to the next, and then on to the next, checking price tags, turning corners of the rugs to see their backs and then spinning on to the next rug. This was a startling departure from the ways of most customers.

9

Most of them hoped to be invisible so as not to be pounced on by a clerk. They tiptoed; they hid behind partitions; they avoided making eye contact. Or they were the other kind, the ones who immediately sought him out and began describing the rugs they had just bought from other dealers.

Here are the impressions that crowded Holden's edgy mind as he eyed the super-charged stranger: "The man is going to spin around and kill me with some sharp instrument. He loves my rugs and is going to buy the lot. He is crazy. He is on drugs and is dangerous. He is a competitor come to check out what I have so he can put me out of business." The aggregate of these impressions sent a powerful dose of adrenaline through his system and soon the customer had Holden's complete attention.

"God damn, man!" the fellow cracked the silence, still without looking at him. "Lock 'em up!"

Holden would not have been more astonished if a racing car had blown through his showroom window. The man's voice *vrooomed* like an eight cylinder hotrod, even though its owner stood no higher than five feet and four inches. "Lock 'em *up!*" the man howled again. Later, Holden believed that in that moment, while his hair stood on end, he had foreseen it all—trouble, joy, more trouble, fun, salvation, trouble.

The man before him stared disagreeably at Holden through narrowed, smoldering eyes, then shouted. "You're *giving* them away, man!" Holden jumped back. "Don't sell them!" the man shouted. "Lock them *up!*" He was perhaps 50 years old and wore a beret, a silk scarf and tasteful, tweedy pants and a white shirt, all of which looked slept in. Altogether, he had an air of shabby nobility, like a dispossessed Russian prince from a time when nobles were no taller than sprites. He was handsome but his looks were troubling. The deep wrinkles in his face suggested a lifetime of judging people harshly. His voice was Homeric, heroic, huge, epic. "Look at this Kazak, man. Look at it! Turkish Kazak you call it? Call it *majesty*, call it *Mohammad*, call it *wisdom*, but don't, for God's sake, sell it for a piddling little five hundred dollars! Get it out of here, man, *hide* it before someone *buys* it." All of this was spoken and shouted and sung in a gorgeously sounded British accent. British? Was that right? Upper-crust Australian? Something vaguely British-Empire.

Holden turned again to his Turkish Kazak, the rug he had been staring at just minutes before. It *was* special. There was strength in it, colors that made him feel like diving in. Had he ever noticed the polish of its wool? It was good to find someone who appreciated it, but who was this man?

"Publish, publish, publish!" The wizened little fellow seemed more and more wound up.

"What?" Holden dared.

"Write about it, man! An article, a book, a course, a philosophy! Pho-to-graph-it-and-*pub*-lish..." and here he turned to look directly at Holden and his voice dropped low, "...or parish."

Holden wondered whether he had just received a death threat. Strangely, though, he was thrilled, because suddenly he could imagine himself writing beautifully about his Kurd Kazak. He would take note of its structure, gaze at its fibers under a powerful microscope, count its natural dyes and take an expert's guess as to its age and origins, and he would report his conclusions to avid readers. But finally he would have to admit that the rug's power and magic were

11

unexplainable. He would write a caption for the page-sized color plate: "To understand the mystery of this rug is to understand the nature of beauty." Or something like that; he would have to work it out.

But now the man spun to face an Afshar bag face with a saturated madder red field, a small piece about 3 feet square and probably Holden's oldest rug, from maybe 1860. The fellow glanced at its price tag and his look became savage. "And for this Afshar—than which I have seen none better—you are asking the price of a rusted and broken twen-ty-five-year-old *Volkswagon*! You're mad! $850!" Holden would have agreed that his price was too low if he had been able to get a word in. God, maybe he *should* lock them up. Or at least publish.

"Uh, my name is Holden Carter." Holden stuck out his hand.

"Deane here," the man said and gave him a perfunctory shake, and then he seemed to lose heart and he sagged. The change was so sudden and dramatic that Holden looked around for a chair and wheeled his own to where the deflated sprite now leaned against a wall. The fellow collapsed into it and shook his head as if bewildered.

"Uh, would that be your first name or your last name? Deane, I mean."

"Avery Deane. You've heard of me." Holden thought maybe he had, but he wasn't sure. "I've just come from London and New York. I bought a silk Kirman at Sotheby's in London. Can I ask them to send it here?"

"No, that's fine," Holden said ambiguously. He had never heard of a silk Kirman—as opposed to a wool one—but he didn't want to admit it. "Kirman" is a Persian name, the name of a city in Eastern Iran in which carpets are woven in a fine city-style. In the West it is most often pronounced **Ker** m'n, as if it were a town somewhere near Fresno. But the Persians pronounce it something like Khyr **mahn**. Deane pronounced it the Persian way. Holden noticed that his voice still rang beautifully though he now seemed sapped of strength or perhaps was discouraged or possibly was ill and feverish or withdrawing from some illegal drug. Anyway, Holden was relieved that the man had stopped shouting. He didn't know what might have happened if the fellow had kept whirling around.

"You don't know what you have here, do you?" Deane sounded to Holden as if he were trying to keep calm. "They don't have rugs like these in London. They don't have rugs like these in New York or Salzburg or Paris. That's because *you* have them all here in this..." Avery looked around at the 600-foot showroom.

"Surely he must have guessed that I live in the back," Holden thought, embarrassed.

"...here in this piddling little hole and you're doing your best to give them away." Uh oh. Deane was getting wound up again.

"So you think my prices are too low?"

At this, the little man with a big voice sprang out of his chair and roared, "Lock 'em *up*, man, you're *giving* them away!"

Chapter Two

Years ago he had discovered that the cheapest way to appear wealthy without being wealthy was to drive a vintage Porsche 928.

Avery Deane was thinking about a rumor he was chasing—that the San Francisco Museum wished to acquire a Ching Dynasty Dragon rug. Absorbed by the thought, he ran a red light and was pulled over by a Berkeley policeman.

Through his open window, Avery boomed, "By God, sir, what is that you're driving? A Crown Victoria? Under all those bells and whistles? Flashing lights? Excellent choice, sir!"

The policeman, a tall, clean-shaven fellow, glanced at his patrol car as if he had never before thought about what it was. "It's just a Ford, but they've got 'em souped up. Uh, sir, did you know that you just drove through a red light, traveling 23 miles an hour?"

Deane seemed amazed. "I don't know how you do it! Radar, is that it? High tech, by God. High tech police work."

"How we do what, sir?"

"23 miles an hour, man! You had me timed exactly!"

"We try, sir."

"Well, I've been trying to get the hang of driving in the States, and, just between you and me, I don't know how you do it."

"How we do what, sir"

"Drive on the wrong side of the road!" Deane erupted in laughter. The young cop grinned.

"Hey, I wondered about that accent, sir. I guess where you're from they drive on the other side of the road."

Still smiling, Avery Deane shook his head as if in wonderment and said, "Can you imagine how hard it is to get used to driving on the other side of the road? I say! Well, have they tightened up the suspension on those Crown Victorias of yours? You must have to do some very critical driving in them."

"Critical?"

"No margin for error when you're chasing a perp, right? Bloody cars have to respond!"

"I'd say so. Sir, may I see your driver's license?"

"Hah! You got me! Up against the wall, feet spread and all that, huh? I don't have one!"

"You don't have a driver's license?"

"In this country. In my country I have a bloody commercial license. I am allowed by law to drive any vehicle with up to sixteen wheels."

"Are you just touring, sir? What is your country?"

"By God, man, you get right at it! What is my country! I love it right here! Most spectacular land I've ever seen. Golden Gate Bridge, University of California, Albany."

"Albany? You like Albany?"

"Named after my mother's father and his father and his father before him, Lord Albany."

15

The young policeman straightened up. He had been bending over and talking into the foreigner's window the whole time. Then he leaned back into his job. "Well then I guess you are a tourist and won't be needing to get a California drivers license. Sir, I want you to be very careful about not going through stoplights. You must come to a complete stop. And watch that you keep on the right side of the road." He grinned.

Avery smiled, too. "Mia culpa," he said and touched his forehead with the first two fingers of his right hand. "Mia culpa."

"Mia culpa, sir," the young man answered, touching his own forehead, "and have a good time while you're visiting Berkeley. And Albany."

Avery shook his head approvingly, restarted his Porsche and feathered his way down the block.

Years ago he had discovered that the cheapest way to appear wealthy without being wealthy was to drive a vintage Porsche 928. The whole world recognized these as fine, expensive automobiles, yet they represented a terrific buying-opportunity. They had the world's worst resale value. On reaching San Francisco he had purchased a 1968 Porsche for $3500...or, rather, he had traded a rug said to be worth that much for a Porsche. (It was he, of course, who had said the rug was worth $3500.) Only an experienced owner—and Avery was one, having owned a series of them—would have recognized that the automobile was looking death in the eye. Some time ago it had arrived at that stage when the repairs it needed totaled more than the car had sold for, new. It looked like a million dollars, though.

A block down the street now, with the tall policeman barely visible in his rear view mirror, Avery gunned the engine. It *hrummed* the way 8-cylinder Porsches do, as it hurled him down the street toward a stop light. His brakes slowed the car enough so that, when he shot through the red light, laughing like a mad man, he was doing no more than fifty miles per hour.

At lunch, Avery considered his options. Should he eat with the "Website Strategy Group" or the "Western Nurseryman's Association?" Each group offered its members a buffet lunch after its morning meeting, but on the nurseryman's buffet table he saw large stainless steel containers perched over low flames, a sign of hot food. Good. He mingled with the nurserymen as they left their last meeting of the morning and was third in line to wend his way around the table. First, a hot roll and butter, then fried chicken and the other usual buffet fare. Once set up at his table, he came back for a cup of coffee.

Of course in a situation like this, it was clothes, not the automobile, that made the man, so, as he sat down to lunch and coffee, he left his silk scarf around his neck. A scarf gave him an air of dash and style, he believed, and seemed to suggest money. Further, a large scarf was useful for covering clothing that may have become crumpled from infrequent laundering. A scarf and a hat. Most often he wore a beret made from English tweed. No matter where he found himself, people seemed to assume that he was from somewhere in the British Empire and that he was the sporting type or at least the motoring type and that he was moneyed. And every group that he mingled with at lunchtime, such as the nurserymen here in northern California, was delighted to find that at least one of their members had class.

"Civilized," Avery thought as he buttered his roll and peered around the hotel's high-ceilinged Jade Room. Touring Berkeley in his Porsche, he had caught glimpses of a soaring white structure in the foothills above town, and he had been drawn to it by his taste for fine things. Finally he had crested a hill and there, as if at the end of a rainbow, lay a splended white castle surrounded by gardens and tennis courts. The fabulous Claremont Hotel.

Avery returned to the buffet for desert and chose a fruit something-or-other topped by a crumbly crust, brown sugar and a dollop of sour cream. He thought about the little rug store he had happened on that morning. "Poor lad," he said to himself. "Doesn't know what he has." He looked around at the nurserymen at nearby tables. Some looked shockingly like the homeless he had seen on the streets of San Francisco. Their skin was tanned like tree bark from weeding, seeding, feeding and watering their plants in the sun and wind. He shuddered. "Why would they do that to themselves," he wondered. Many of the things people did puzzled him. He wondered whether he should have chosen Website Strategy to dine with, instead.

"He'll be useful, though," Avery said to himself, thinking again about Holden Carter and his inventory of antique rugs. "Maybe I can sell him the silk Kirman." The "silk Kirman" had already been around the block. Avery had traded it to a fellow named Bob in San Francisco to acquire his current Porsche 928. A few days later Bob had squawked.

"I looked it up. There's no such thing as a silk Kirman. You sold me a bill of goods." A heated discussion followed in which Bob threatened to punch Deane. Finally Deane said, "All right, would you rather have cash than the rug?"

"Yes!"

"Good. I'll sell it for you. No problem."

"You'll sell what for me?"

"The silk Kirman. Give it to me and I'll get cash for it. But it'll take me two weeks."

"Give back the rug?"

"Can't sell it for you unless I have it, now, can I?"

"Hmm. Two weeks?"

"Cash."

"Hmm."

So Bob had given the rug back to Avery to sell for him and now Avery had both the Porsche and the rug. Avery smiled, then he thought he would like to have a glass of wine, and he returned to the buffet table.

"You *are* with the Nurserymen, aren't you sir?" the wine steward asked in a worried tone. Deane gave him a puzzled look. "It's just your name-badge, sir. You don't have one." Deane looked downward to where name-badges are most often pinned. Exploring further, he pulled aside his silk scarf and seemed surprised not to find his name pinned to his shirt.

The wine steward eyed Avery's shirt that had once been white.

Avery looked up at the man hired to pour wine. "You have a good eye, man! Noticed instantly that I didn't have a badge. I've been here all day and had no idea. Never pinned the bloody thing on. Would you mind?"

"Would I mind what?"

"If I can find the bloody thing, would you mind pinning it on my shirt? I have two left hands. I've never got the hang of pinning on these blasted things." Avery began searching for his badge, first in his trouser pockets, examining the contents of each, then patting himself here and there as if the damned badge might be anywhere, in some breast pocket, in his arm pits, behind his neck. The wine pourer peered with distaste at Avery's disreputable shirt.

"Pin it on? You want me to pin it onto your shirt?" The wine pourer was a Croatian immigrant who had been drawn to the Claremont Hotel's white towers by the promise of cleanliness and civility. His eyes were riveted on Avery's shirt, which appeared to have been slept in. Often.

"If you don't mind." Avery patted at himself. "If I can find it."

"Oh don't bother, sir. I'm sure you're fine. Red or white, sir? Would you like to try the chardonnay?"

"Fine, yes, fine." He kept searching, then finally stopped patting himself to accept the glass of chardonnay. "Bloody embarrassing, though."

"No, no. It's fine. Enjoy."

"Well." Walking back to his table on the disappointing carpeting—you would think a hotel of this caliber would have *real* Oriental carpets instead of machine-made fakes—Avery gave one of his back pockets a last slap.

Sitting again at his table, twirling his wine, he thought about what had brought him here to the San Francisco Bay Area. Word had gone out in European rug circles that the San Francisco Museum was interested in acquiring a Chinese dragon rug. Not just any dragon rug, but a particular one, a rug described in the 17ᵗʰ century by a French traveler named Ferrier, who had discovered it in China. Disguised as a Chinese monk, Ferrier had stolen his way into an inner sanctum, a palace within a palace, where he found and later described a knotted rug that was used, he thought, much as altar cloths are used in Western religious ceremonies. It was small—he guessed at 1.5 meters by 3 meters—and he described it as "haunting." A flamboyant, five-toed blue dragon lay on a saffron field. The Frenchman had been mesmerized by the dragon's staring eyes.

Most scholars believed that, if the rug had ever existed at all—that is, if Ferrier had not been lying or exaggerating or romanticizing about it—there was a good chance that it would have been preserved. So-called "inner palace" artifacts from China's Ching Dynasty were famously well preserved. They had been regarded as holy and hence were fanatically well cared for by the monks to whom they had been entrusted. Other inner palace woolen carpets had come down through the centuries intact, if sometimes discolored and battered. So there was reason to hope that the Ferrier rug might turn up someday.

That was the rug the San Francisco Museum was seeking to acquire. Of course, all museums sought to acquire the Ferrier Dragon Rug, as it had come to be called. What was remarkable now was that the San Francisco Museum was offering a million dollars for it. Or, at least, that was the rumor.

"A noble figure," Avery thought. "It would be amusing to secure the Ferrier dragon rug for the San Francisco Museum, wouldn't it—even if I have to weave it myself? Of course, I don't know what the rug looks like. But, then, neither does the museum. Which is really quite convenient, when you consider."

Avery had enjoyed his chardonnay. It soothed him, but, alas, it was now gone. He eyed the buffet table where the wine pourer was still pouring.

Tomorrow morning at 11 o'clock he would meet with the curator of Oriental Rugs and Carpets at the San Francisco Museum, Sarah Atwood. But right now he thought it would be nice to have another glass of chardonnay. He liked the hotel and thought it might be a good place to stay for a while. He would have to work out something about the money. But first, wine. He stood and headed toward the wine, patting his pockets.

Chapter Three

"But what is the top of the Oriental rug world?"
she asked herself.

 There came a time in Sarah Atwood's life when she had to decide what to do with the rest of it. At 34, she had no profession except as a successful corporate wife, and that had ended suddenly when her marriage had failed. She received a sizable alimony which she believed was inadequate. In addition, she had the house—an impressive brownstone in Georgetown, a collection of fine furniture including several very expensive Oriental carpets, and undeniable social graces, including good looks and expensive-looking hair. She was at the height of her powers and hungry for more money.

It occurred to Sarah to return to school for a degree that might earn a good job, but that seemed such a long way around. In fact, no job or profession came to mind that did sound good to her. Rather, her impulse was to have some kind of commercial relationship with the finer things of life, like yachts, for instance, or Bentleys. Or Oriental carpets. Carpets came to mind simply because she walked on a couple of good ones every day.

She pictured a business card:

Sarah Atwood
Oriental Carpets

It was all too vague, though, wasn't it? She would not attract money with a card like that. Unsatisfied, Sarah began spending hours each day staring at her Oriental rugs. She would walk from one large room to another, peering at them as they lay spread on cherry-wood floors. But, rather than studying their charming colors or their powerful designs, she was searching them for a business plan. In fact, she had no interest at all in the carpets except to speculate what she might be able to sell them for.

It was Sarah's belief that, whatever she did, she should shoot for the top. "But what *is* the top of the Oriental rug world?" she asked herself as she stared at her carpets. "I have to know what the top is before I can set my sights on it." She knew there were upper-end rug dealers who were fabulously wealthy. Is that where she should aim?

Sarah Atwood
Fine Antique Carpets
By appointment

But one needed *decades* to arrive at the top of that heap, plus, she guessed, genuine expertise. She thought she could fake the expertise, but she could not bare the thought of spending years and years gathering the inventory of antique rugs she would need to reach the top. No, that path was too slow. Should she import new Oriental rugs?

Sarah Atwood
Importer of Fine Oriental Rugs

But the thought of traveling in dangerous countries which were sure to be dirty disturbed her. No, not an importer. Then a writer about Oriental rugs? No money in it. "Follow the money," she thought. "Where are the most valuable carpets in the world right this minute? In collections?" She considered. "No,in museums." That insight caused Sarah a measure of satisfaction. Museums.

Sarah Atwood
Curator, Oriental Rugs and Carpets
National Carpet Museum
Washington, DC

She pictured her card in tasteful shades of ecru and ivory, and she liked what she saw. She imagined herself in charge of the oldest and finest and most valuable rugs in the world. She had a premonition of opportunities, misty in detail now, but promising. She had found the top of the heap. The question now was how to reach it. As she turned to that question, she paced from one of her carpets to another, staring without seeing. It was unlikely that she could become a curator over night, she reasoned, but on the other hand she wasn't willing to spend *years* to reach her goal. She would have to find a way to move things along. In the mean time, why not call herself a consultant. "Consultant" had a nice ring.

Sarah Atwood
Oriental Carpet Consultant

Good, yet her instinct told her something was missing. She needed credibility. Like maybe:

Sarah Atwood
Oriental Carpet Consultant
By Appointment by Her Majesty, the Queen

Something like that. "How stupid that we don't have queens!" she thought. She would have to find some other way.

....

Ruggies stood in circles, swirling drinks. They milled about on a wonderful carpet, a 14 by 20-foot Serapi with colors and wool that sparkled after 100 years underfoot, but they ignored it. It was large rather than small, and hence it was thought by them to have been woven for commerce and therefore not collectible. Rather, they judged it to be *decorative*.

A fundamental tenant of all rug collectors is that some rugs are collectible and others are not. Oh, collectors disagree about whether Turkish or Caucasian or Chinese rugs or rugs from East Turkestan are the most collectible. Some prefer rugs from the south of Persia, others from the north of Africa. But all agree that, to be collectible, a rug has to be *old* and it *must not have been woven to sell.* If it was woven to sell, *collectors will not buy it.* Or if it was woven to sell, its weaver must have been forced by poverty to sell it for staples, like salt or grain, and, even then, it must have been sold long ago. It was clear to all who partied on it that the splendid Serapi had not been woven for salt money.

One of the circles of rug-people was discussing fakes.

"Luckily there aren't many in our field. I believe I've never seen one."

"That's why they're called fakes, Kyle, because you don't know one when you see one. Believe me, you've seen fakes." The others in the circle smiled. That exchange was between two of the rug-world's titans: Kyle Berman, director of Washington's National Carpet Museum and the young archeologist and rug-writer, Marley Phillips III.

"Seriously, Kyle," Phillips continued, "there may be more fakes in our field than you think. Has it ever occurred to you that your celebrated Ninth Star Kazak is a fake? Or your famous Arabachi engsi?" Not only Berman but everyone in the circle frowned, signaling that perhaps some things are not to be joked about. The Ninth Star Kazak and the Arabachi, fakes? They were among the cornerstones of the museum's collection, and Kyle Berman had personally authorized buying them at auction for a combined $210,000.

Young Holden Carter was a witness to this conversation. At that time he was a student—a candidate for a master's degree in art history—and a rug collector but not yet a dealer. Though he stood *with* the titans, he was far from one of them. He was astonished by the suggestion that his favorite rug in the world, the so-called Ninth Star Kazak, might be a fake. For decades no more than eight star Kazaks were known to exist. Then, just a few years ago, a ninth piece had surfaced near London, and it was the best of them all. Director Berman of The National Carpet Museum had acquisitioned it.

Holden had been pleasantly surprised a month earlier when he had received an invitation to today's reception. At home in Berkeley, he had opened a hand-written invitation to a reception in Washington, DC in connection with an exhibition of rugs at the National Carpet Museum. The person inviting him, a Sarah Atwood, whose name he didn't recognize, said that the National Carpet Museum's Kyle Berman would be attending, as well as a number of other famous rug figures, Marley Phillips among them. Holden had made the *haj* to Washington, of course, flattered by the invitation and eager to meet his rug heroes. And now here he was, listening to rug-talk that seemed, to him, to shimmer like precious stones.

"Oh bosh, Marley! That's nonsense," said Charles Francis Green. Green was America's most famous rug scholar, said to have handled, photographed and analyzed every important rug and carpet in every museum in the world, and to have a dossier on each one. "They are no more fakes than I am."

Phillips laughed. "Well, we'll never know, will we, since the Carpet Museum won't give me a crack at them? How about it Kyle, are you willing to give me a two-hour examination with each of them plus a few tiny samples of their dyes and material? Something tells me those rugs aren't what they seem to be."

Berman looked uncomfortable. "We've talked about this before. I would have to secure the approval of the Board of

Directors. I imagine some of them might prefer to let well enough alone." Holden had the impression that Berman felt that way himself.

"Let well enough alone is *right*!" Old Ulysses Pope spoke for the first time. Holden knew him to be the country's preeminent Oriental rug collector, a famously wealthy and crusty industrialist from North Carolina. "You just want to debunk something, Phillips; put a feather in your cap and then leave rug collectors and museums all over the world afraid to buy anything because it might be a fake. You're damned destructive, let me tell you."

"But how can you possibly fake a rug, anyway? You mean make a new one look like an antique?" Holden asked. The others ignored him. Actually, hard feelings made him uncomfortable and he had hoped by his questions to defuse the tension welling up among his heroes in the circle. But before Phillips, the archeologist, could answer Pope, a woman approached the group with an elegant hand extended toward Kyle Berman for a shake.

"Thank you so much for coming, Mr. Berman, Mr. Phillips, Mr. Pope, Mr. Green and..." She looked briefly at Holden and nodded. Kyle Berman shook hands with her and so did the others. Holden mumbled a hello.

To Holden, the woman had the unmistakable aura of a society lady. He recognized the aura even though he had never before been in its presence. Her hair was streaked blond and palomino, her clothes were tasteful, her manners easy and her smile was self-assured. She was a society lady, but not a society matron, Holden thought, not at all. She was only a few years older than him, and she was very good to look at. The lady chatted easily with the circle for a few moments and then moved on to the next.

When she was gone, Pope said, "Who the devil is she? She's goddamned good looking." Holden thought he heard lechery in the rich old man's tone, and perhaps disrespect, and he disapproved. For his part, Holden felt quite a swelling of respect for her. As she glided away from the group to the next one, Holden's eyes followed.

"I assume she's our hostess," Berman said, "but I can't think of her name."

"Sarah Atwood," Phillips said. "I researched her after I received her invitation, or I tried to, anyway. I couldn't find out much about her."

"Sarah Atwood," Holden said to himself, "the woman who sent me an invitation."

"I didn't know her either," Berman said, "and the only reason I came was because she promised that you gentlemen would be here." He nodded at all of them except Holden.

"Strange," Phillips said. "my invitation she said that *you* would be here, Kyle. Well, I guess she was right." They laughed.

"So we're all here," Charles Francis Green said, "and yet not one of us have met her before or knows who she is."

"Well," Holden said, "I guess we do now. Sarah Atwood." But again no one appeared to have noticed his existence. He was as invisible to the others as the gorgeous old Serapi underfoot.

Less than a week later, Sarah picked up her new business cards. She left them in their box until much later that night when she had made herself comfortable. Finally she put down her glass of port and, sitting with one leg tucked beneath her, she opened the little box and pulled out a card. She had indeed opted for ecru and ivory, and rather than the usual rug motifs that most rug-people work into their business cards, she had only simple, formal lettering followed by her phone number.

Ms. Sarah Atwood,
Oriental Rug Consultations
In Cooperation with Mr. Charles Francis Green

Sarah smiled at her tasteful new business card. "There's no harm in claiming cooperation with the most respected rug scholar in the land—or any law against it. Anyway, he'll never see the cards, and something tells me he won't make a fuss if he does. Charlie Green is a gentleman."

She did an easy calculation: $8000 for the catered reception, $45 for the business cards. $8045. "I made 50 friends in the right places and saved 5 to 8 years in my climb to the top. Charlie Green may not be the Queen, but...I'm on my way." Sarah raised her glass and toasted herself.

The following Monday, someone from the National Carpet Museum invited Sarah to a "Show-and-Tell" at the museum. "Please bring a favorite rug and be prepared to share your knowledge about it with fellow rug connoisseurs."

This was to be her first public appearance as a rug expert. She looked up one of the DC rug dealers she had invited to the reception and from him bought a tribal rug called a Belouch. When she showed him her card he said, "You work with Charles Green?" She said, "Yes," and he sold her the rug for half-price.

Next she called Charles Francis Green. "Mr. Green, I wonder if you would look at a Belouch in my collection and advise me about it?" He invited her to bring it by his comfortable old home. In person, he thanked her again for her wonderful party, told her how happy he was to have met her and said he would be delighted to advise her about her rug. He was very attentive. He told her what was good about her Belouch and what wasn't so good, so that after a while she knew exactly what she would say at the show-and-tell. (She would tell her "fellow rug-lovers" that, instead of bringing her best rug, she had brought "the first rug I ever bought. I would like to share with you some of the lessons I learned from it.") Before she left Green's home, she thanked him for his cooperation.

"Cooperation?" He looked puzzled.

"Yes," she said, "I appreciate it."

She did not leave him with one of her new business cards.

Chapter Four

Of course, it is open to question whether any Oriental rug can properly be called a work of art.

 Sarah's 14 by 20-foot Serapi, on which rug fanciers partied without paying it any mind, was conceived in northwestern Iran in about 1890 and was woven not long afterwards in a rural area further north and east. Here is the story of how it came into existence.

After the disruptive Afghan invasion of the Persian Empire in 1722, rug weaving in Persia went into a 150-year-long tailspin. It was not until about 1880 that an industry was reborn, and when it was, it was driven by the rug merchants of Tabriz in the northwest of Iran. The Turkish-speaking weavers of Tabriz produced fine and elaborate carpets in formal, flowing, court designs. Faced with more demand than they could supply, Tabrizi merchants commissioned weavers in nearby villages to make carpets after designs they supplied. In particular they commissioned rugs to be made in Heriz and in several smaller villages near Heriz, including one called Serapi. However, the weavers of the Heriz district were unused to weaving such finely knotted carpets and unused to working from drawings. They were intimidated but resourceful. Unwilling to give up lucrative orders from Tabriz, weavers strung their looms and began working. Of course they had to simplify designs in order to accommodate their more modest weaving skills and in order to weave from memory rather than graph-paper "cartoons." What they produced was not at all what the Tabrizi merchants had expected. Heriz-district weavers created rugs so distinct and different from Tabriz carpets that they could not be sold as a Tabriz. They could only be named after the villages in which they were woven, such as Heriz, Goravan, Ahar and Serapi. Thus were born, almost by accident, what many connoisseurs today believe to be works of art, one of the earliest and best of which was Sarah Atwood's Serapi.

Of course, it is open to question whether any Oriental rug can properly be called a work of art, especially one woven by three or four weavers sitting side by side at the loom, a rug whose design and colors were plotted not by its weavers but by institute-trained designers from far away. Or, another way to think of it is, can a translation be a work of art—a translation, in this case, from a Tabriz to a Heriz? Craft may be a better word for the process than art Still, something creative was stirred up in this marriage of Tabriz designer and Serapi weaver. No one who opens his or her senses to Sarah's Serapi (as opposed to merely standing on it and swirling cocktails) would deny it.

Though the rug gives the impression of balance and harmony, there is no exact repetition in it from side to side or end to end. Each of its several weavers has contributed a quirky use of color or a unique ornament that is never again found in the rug. Somehow, within the confines of a design put up by a merchant some kilometers distant, and working to produce an article whose sole reason for being is that it will be offered for sale, each weaver makes the carpet a personal expression.

Sarah was not the Serapi's first owner. In 1900, it sold to a 45 year old couple for the polished hardwood floors of their new home in Alameda, California. Alameda is an island in the San Francisco Bay, close enough to San Francisco so that even in 1900 a trip there took less than a day, but far enough from San Francisco to enjoy somewhat different weather. Wealthy San Franciscans sometimes built second homes in an Alameda neighborhood called the Gold Coast and enjoyed warmer, less-foggy summers there. The house, a large Victorian, cost $7,500 to build, and the Serapi cost nearly 13% as much, $950. It was very expensive. The couple loved the bold carpet because its strong, saturated colors and its vigorous design. It seemed to capture the spirit of a country house, and they summered their family on its comfortable wool pile, its cheerful colors and its simple geometric lines. When a daughter inherited it in 1930, it was just beginning to come into its full beauty. Its natural dyes had softened subtly and the Serapi's good Persian wool had acquired a luster from use. Unfortunately, the daughter was unable to fit the over-sized carpet into any room in her home and made an unwise trade with a San Francisco rug dealer for a new carpet that did fit her space. Even though the Depression was still raging, the rug dealer managed to sell the piece for $1250 to a New York rug dealer who traveled the States looking for just such semi-antique carpets. The New York dealer must have had times when he believed he had paid too much for it, because it sat in his Manhattan showroom for five years. During that time it was opened for customers so seldom that eventually it was attacked by moths and required $150 of re-knotting. But finally a fifty-year-old bachelor who produced nationally syndicated radio programs purchased the Serapi for his large Manhattan flat and he paid the impressive sum of $3500. The sensitive, artistic crowd who gathered there regarded it as astonishingly beautiful, and one friend, an oil painter with a national reputation, was so influenced by it that his sense of color was forever after influenced by it. In 1952 the radio producer who owned the Serapi suffered a stroke and died. Though he had no immediate heirs, he had a nephew in Maryland, and to the nephew he bequeathed his earthly goods. The nephew did have a living room large enough for the carpet. But this was a time when a man's wealth seemed to be measured by the thickness of his wall-to-wall carpeting and Oriental rugs were considered old fashioned. The nephew and his wife stored the Serapi, none too carefully, and never used it. Their daughter, Sarah, inherited it in 1992, when she was 30 years old and the Serapi was 92 years old. When she and her husband opened the carpet to consider using it in their Washington brownstone, it was discovered that rats had nibbled its selvages. Though disgusted, Sarah immediately recognized that the carpet was valuable. The rug dealer who repaired it told her it was worth "about sixty."

"About sixty what?" she asked.

"Not dollars, madam." He sniffed. "And not cents." That became a family story.

At the beginning, Sarah regarded it as something of value and status and as a set of colors she would have to account for in designing her interior. Later she thought she perceived in it a spirit that she should exploit in her interior design. And finally, she came to value it as having influenced the course of her meteoric career. But the truth is that she never came to love it. It was not until the very end that she fell head over heels in love with an Oriental rug.

Chapter Five

The fabled and mythical sum of 'a million dollars!'
There's something so satisfying about it.

 Three years after Sarah Atwood's party in Washington, Avery Deane phoned her at the San Francisco Museum of Fine Arts in San Francisco, where she was now curator of the Carpet and Rug Collection. "Avery Deane?" she asked. "Your name seems familiar." That was a polite way of saying that she couldn't place him.

"You may have read a thing or two that I've written, or you may have read about me. This and that. Here and there. Rugs, of course. That's what I would like to talk with you about." She liked his voice.

"Rugs?"

"The Ferrier Dragon Rug."

"Why don't you stop by the Museum?" she suggested. And he did.

She offered him a private tour of the collection that morning before the Museum opened to the public. She thought he looked like someone who had once been wealthy. After a few turns through the rug galleries with Sarah, he purred, "You're royalty, my dear; a queen admiring her treasure." She may have reminded him of Princess Diana as she guided him through tapestried corridors. Many people had been struck by her lucky resemblance to that lovely woman. And others had told her that she had an air, almost, of owning the rugs in her care. She smiled at Avery, who was barely her height, and asked if he would like to go backstage, so to speak, into the basement storage area of the rug department. Hundreds and hundreds of rugs and carpets—the difference between them, by the way, being only that the small ones are rugs and the larger ones are carpets—were carefully rolled, labeled and protected from vermin of all kinds. There were far more rugs in storage down here than on display upstairs in the galleries. Over the decades, many folks who were enthusiastic about their Oriental rugs had made gifts of their favorites to the Museum, hoping to share them with the public. Fortunately, most such gifts were made posthumously and their former owners never had to know that their beloved rugs—including those that had real merit—would languish forever in the museum's dim storage areas, never to be displayed. Still, Sarah seemed to take an owner's pride even in these rugs few people beyond the hired help were likely ever to see unrolled.

Back in the galleries again and heading with Sarah toward her office, Deane enthused over one antique rug after another, literally singing their praises. As for instance: "Oh Lotto on the wall, *you're* the fairest of them all. A bloody, bloody beaut!" Each old rug seemed to stir him more than the last until finally he seemed to Sarah to have become quite overwrought. As they walked side-by-side, he moved a few quick steps ahead and then turned to stop her. He glowered. "Jealous louts! They'll send hooligans here from all the great museums to slash your rugs! Guard them!" he roared,

"Watch your back!" She whipped her head around but saw nothing threatening. Then his voice dropped conspiratorially. "Post armed men around that Polonaise. Build a moat, woman." Then his voice rose again in volume and pitch. "Lock 'em up!" Sarah was alarmed. Was he mad? Was he going to attack her here in the empty museum? Or was he merely far too enthusiastic about Oriental rugs? She had seen others who had gone off the deep end in their love for them. She waited to see what he might do. He took a deep breath, shook his head and held up one arm as if to say, "Wait, wait, I've gone too far. Please forgive me. I'll settle down." They resumed their stroll toward her office and he was much more docile.

Even during his rant, though, she had loved his voice.

A few minutes later, sitting across from Sarah at her desk, he said, "There's just one thing more you need to put the San Francisco Museum of Fine Arts at the top of the list: The Pope collection."

"Ah," she agreed, "the Pope collection." She smiled. "Ulysses is a friend of mine, so I'm assuming he will leave us everything. After all, what are friends for?" She laughed.

"Everyone else assumes the same thing, you know. Every museum. Pope encourages all of them to believe he will bequeath them his rugs."

"Of course I know that. We all do. But what am I supposed to do? Stop trying? Ulysses has the best collection of Oriental rugs in the world."

"Strange," he said, "but I believe you might land it."

"I've made it my mission." Quite true. It was one thing, she thought, to have become the curator of a good collection of rugs, and it would be quite another matter to be in control of the best collection of Oriental rugs in the country—with an appraised value (if she were to land the Pope rugs) of about $24,000,000. A collection that big and that valuable suggested possibilities.

Sarah's office was exquisitely furnished. Her simple, tasteful old Spanish desk, its original finish full of shallow dents and scratches from two centuries of use, sat on an antique Berber carpet still in decent condition. A mounted pre-Columbian textile hung on a wall near where she sat, radiating glorious color but unraveling around its edges. It seemed to her as if the man across the desk from her was perfectly in place here. His silk scarf was no more or less worn than her Berber rug; his beret was no more or less battered than her desk. What he and her furniture and textiles had in common, she thought, was the mystique and character that time and use bestow on people and furniture and old tools and ox carts and cupboards alike. Of course Deane was hardly antique. Was he fifty? But somehow one had the impression that he was from an ancient line of...what? Of landed gentry? Of Dukes? Earls? From a long line of moneyed people, anyway.

"Mr. Deane, I'm taking too much of your time. How can I help you? On the phone, you mentioned the Ferrier Dragon Rug."

"It's being said that the Museum would like to acquire it. May I ask whether I have heard correctly?"

"It is not the Museum but a private collector who wishes to acquire the rug. I'm trying to help because I would like to see the rug eventually make its way to the Museum's collection, through a donation, of course, since the Museum could never afford to pay for it."

"Yes, that is the other part of what I heard, that a figure of a million dollars is being offered for it. I pray that it's so: the fabled and mythical sum of 'a million dollars!' There's something so satisfying about it." The small man across from her was aglow. His voice rang. "Don't you imagine," he went on, "that, in the movie, the Maltese Falcon must have been worth a million dollars? I don't remember, but I'm sure that was it. That's the figure around which novels and murders are plotted. Things start to *happen* when a million dollars are involved. A million dollars for a rug the size of your tabletop. But is it true? Are the rumors right about the amount of money involved?"

"Where did you hear about that?"

"Everywhere. New York, London, Hamburg."

"And where are you from, if I may ask?"

"Why, I just told you. Everywhere! New York, London, Hamburg! San Francisco, right now."

"And why do you ask about the Ferrier Dragon Rug?"

Deane leaned forward—quite far forward over the desk, really, so that Saraha sensed his breath, which was not unpleasant—and he spoke as if he were sharing a secret in his rich, accented voice. "Wouldn't like to arouse your hopes at this stage, my dear, but I may—and I say only *may*—know approximately where the rug is."

Sarah's face remained impassive. "And where is it?"

"Approximately?"

"Approximately."

"China. That's the problem."

"But not such a problem now, certainly, in this age of fast travel."

"Not it. The problem is getting it out of China where authorities frown on the exportation of antiquities." Avery laughed. "'National treasures,' that's what they call them these days, but I remember when a few pounds could get you out of China with a 4000 year old bronze."

"Well, you're right," Sarah said. "I'd rather not become acquisitive about a rug I can't have. It brings something out in me that's not at all nice. Let's not talk about it again until you have something substantial to report, all right? Now, am I right in thinking that you are in the rug business? You certainly know rugs, but I don't remember hearing your name in rug circles."

"Haven't heard my name? Of course not. They pay me extra to be anonymous."

"I beg your pardon?"

"I'm a ghostwriter, my dear. I write for others who sign their names to my work. I'm one of that brotherhood of writers paid to be ghosts: unknown, invisible ghosts."

"How interesting! May I ask what you've written? Do you write about rugs?"

"My lips are sealed. Can't in good conscience tell you. Breach of contract, my dear."

"Hmm. Where do you work? Somewhere in the British Empire I would guess."

"Anywhere I am. San Francisco at the moment, the San Francisco Museum of Fine Arts."

"What an interesting man," she thought. "If I can believe him. But how can anyone tell whether he's what he says he is: a ghost?" He was handsome, she thought, but for a pinch of impatience around his mouth and a certain suggestion in his looks that he might explode at any moment. "Small man, big voice," she said to herself. But the charm of his big, round, ringing voice was not to be under-estimated. And it was not just his voice. His beautiful elocution and his refined accent were charming, too.

"But, my dear, before we leave the subject entirely," he said, "would you care to say whether the figure I spoke of was correct? And may I ask who the collector is that would like to acquire it?"

"My lips are sealed," she smiled. "He or she wishes to remain anonymous. And do you mean *approximately* how much would the collector pay for the Ferrier Dragon Rug—since you are speaking only of its approximate location?"

"Well, yes, that would be fine."

"Then, yes, approximately one million dollars. But since the rug you're teasing me with is locked up in China, let's just forget about it. Let us change the subject."

"You're just like me, my dear," he answered. "If there's anything people like us—in love with art—if there's anything we despise, it's money. We won't talk about it again until we have to."

Sarah smiled and made a motion that meant she was zipping her lips.

Chapter Six

"Shame on you!" she hissed.
*"Just *shame*!" as if he were a bad dog.*

 When stout old Ulysses Pope walked in, Holden, recognized him immediately, not only from having stood in a social circle with him at a reception several years earlier in Sarah Atwood's party in Georgetown, but also from the many photos of the famous collector he had seen in rug magazines over the years. Holden sprang up from where he had been sitting at his roll-top desk and rushed to welcome the great man to his rug store.

"Sir! Mr. Pope! Glad you could make it! I mean, I'm happy you could come!"

The old Southern gentleman looked startled. "Were you expecting me?"

"No, no, I just mean that I'm glad to see you, sir. I wasn't expecting you at all."

The famous man frowned. "Did I come at a bad time?"

Holden blushed. "Good heavens, no. I just mean to say welcome to my store, such as it is."

Pope looked around. "Is there something wrong with it? It's damned small, of course. Is that what you mean?" He glanced at the curtained door at the rear of the shop. "God, I hope you don't *live* back there." Pope looked at him with an expression of distaste, as if he had just learned that Holden did things to children. Holden blushed, but before he could deny or affirm that he lived in the rear of his store, Pope asked, "What's this?" He tottered over to the Turkish Kazak, the unusual rug Holden had bought at the flea market. But Holden had slipped into a kind of twilight zone and stood flat-footed, unable to respond. He was washed by a strange feeling that all of this was unreal. First, just days before, Avery Deane had showed up in his shop and had gone right to the same Kazak, and now the country's most famous rug collector had walked in and was stroking its wool and turning a corner to examine its back. What was happening? And all of this after years of being the rug world's best-kept secret.

"Mr. Pope," he said rapturously, "you may not remember, sir, but we have met before." Pope seemed uninterested. "Remember a reception in Washington, DC about three years ago? It was in connection with an exhibition at the National Carpet Museum. You and Charles Francis Green and Marley Phillips and Kyle Berman were there. We talked about rug fakes, and Sarah Atwood introduced herself. I remember that you commented on her great beauty. My name is Holden Carter." He wondered whether he should hold out his hand for a shake, but Pope made no response at all. It was as if Holden had not spoken.

But still, Holden was gratified when the collector asked him soon after, "What do you make this out to be?"

"Well," Holden thought, "at least he's asking my opinion about a rug. That's something." He remembered Deane saying to him about the same rug, 'Call it *majesty*, call it *Mohammad*, call it *wisdom*, but don't, for God's sake, sell it

46

for a piddling little five hundred dollars!' Aloud he said, "My guess is it was made by Kurds near Kars, where Turkey, Iran and the Caucasus share a border. I'm calling it a Kurd Kazak or a Turkish Kazak or sometimes even a Kars Kazak. Last quarter of the 19th century." If Pope had any thoughts, he kept them to himself and tottered around the shop looking at rugs on the walls. He looked old but no older than the last time Holden had seen him, though the man had to be in his mid-eighties. He could hardly believe that the man who was said to have the best private collection of rugs in the world was in his store and taking his rugs seriously. Pope made his way from one rug to the next like a bee buzzing from one flower to the other—and finally he returned to the Kurdish Kazak.

"How much do you want for this one?" Holden thought the question was academic because he couldn't imagine Pope actually buying something from him.

"Oh it's on the tag." Actually, Holden was too embarrassed to say the price out loud. After Avery Deane had been in and had roared at him to raise his prices, Holden, feeling giddy for a day or two, had raised the price of the Kazak from $500 to $750. But Pope would not look at the price tag. Instead, he turned to look at Holden, and his expression said that he knew and Holden knew that the price tag had no bearing on anything and what, after all, was the real and actual price? For the first time it occurred to him that Pope might be interested in buying it. For some reason the thought embarrassed him. "Well, Mr. Pope, I would be happy to see it in your collection. It's $500." Pope stared at him and continued to stare at him and his eyes narrowed and his mouth turned down. Holden was so uncomfortable that he could hardly catch his breath. "Do you think that's too much, Mr. Pope?" Pope held his gaze. "Uh, how about $400?" Holden asked. Pope nodded. The bargain was struck.

"Wrap it for me. I'll take it and my man will send a check." As Holden took the rug off the wall, he found that his hands were shaking. He had just sold a rug to Ulysses Pope. Or at least he hoped so.

"My man?" he wondered. "My man will send the check?"

"Do you drive, young man? Would you care to have lunch?"

"Well yes, I'd like to. Thank you Mr. Pope. I really love to drive. I could drive us both!" The old man looked at him. "I mean, where would you like to eat?"

"Wherever they make good cocktails."

"Cocktails! Of course. Good cocktails." The truth is that Holden was in the dark about cocktails. He knew restaurants that served good coffee and baked great pies, and he knew the places that had good imported beer, and he knew a little about wine. But cocktails? Also—something that he didn't want to mention—he felt really strange closing his store in the middle of the day to go out for lunch. He always just ducked through the curtained door and whipped up a sandwich. He considered making up a sign to stick on his window: CLOSED FOR EMERGENCY. BACK AT 3. But wouldn't it seem strange that, if it were an emergency, he would know when he would be back? Lying always confused him. So in the end he just locked up and he and Ulysses Pope got in Pope's big rented Lincoln and Holden started the engine.

Suddenly he had an idea. "Uh, how do you like seafood, Mr. Pope?"

"Fine."

"Well then, I know just the place. It's at the marina. Uh, I forget the name right now. Great cocktails, though!"

"Fine."

Holden drove the gigantic Lincoln with terrified care, so nervous that he could hardly see straight. On the city streets he had no feel in the big car for how close he was to other cars, and on a brief stretch of freeway he felt no connection with the road at all, and it seemed to him that the car might float right off the highway. Even now it was drifting to the right so that its tires set up a rapid bump-a-ta, bump-a-ta, bump-a-ta sound as they shuddered over the lane markers. Pope didn't seem to notice, though.

"How would you like to take me around, after lunch, young man?"

"Take you around, sir?" He struggled to pull the automobile back into his lane but over-corrected and was out of control for a full two or three seconds.

"Yes, take me around."

"Well sure. Anything I can do for you. Like, you mean, take you around to..." Pope didn't say. "Just here and there, huh? Sure, I'd be glad to."

The minute they pushed open the big, glass door, Holden remembered something about the restaurant from the one time he had been there, a long time before. The waitresses wore little playboy bunny costumes—not like real bunnies with ears, but really, really short skirts and fishnet stockings and tops that were like *dirndels*, where the waitresses' chests

49

were pushed out or up or however that worked. And they had little white puff-ball tails. That's why he thought of them as bunny costumes. "Ha ha!" he said to Pope. "Well, I guess there's an *Austrian* theme here or something. We forgot to wear our *lederhosen*! Ha ha!" Mr. Pope slowly turned and looked at him for a moment and then began staring at the waitresses. He and Holden were showed to their table by a wonderful bunny whose long, thin neck and pronounced collar bones seemed not to go with her fleshy bosom. Once seated, Holden found a little green glass cup full of pretzel sticks and peanuts and other things that looked familiar, and he began nibbling them. He was surprised by how dim the light was, almost as if it were midnight.

Soon another bunny came to their table and asked if they would like to order drinks. Pope ordered a martini, exchanging a few words with the buxom young woman, like "over" and something about onions and vodka. The girl turned to Holden, who happened to know something about how to order a martini. "A martini please," he said, "your house gin, dry, straight up." He got the words out.

She was really quite pretty with her chest so white. "Oliver Twist?" she said to him and seemed to be expecting an answer.

Strangely, Holden had re-read the book just recently and had had a lot of thoughts about it, like how amazingly fresh it seemed. "Fresh" as in *not-dated*. So when the waitress said Oliver Twist to him as if it were a question, Holden had his second episode of *deja vu* that day. Suddenly, again, nothing seemed real: the waitress asking him about Charles Dickens, the midnight light at noon, his lunch companion, Ulysses Pope, the bunnies. So, really, he just shut down, as if all his nerves had gone on strike. Still, he was aware that the pretty girl remained standing by his side, waiting for him to say something or do something.

After some time, Pope, staring at him, asked, "Do you want an olive or a twist of lemon?"

As if from the edge of an epileptic seizure, Holden was recalled to life, called back to the here and now, strange as it was, and he said "Olive," and suddenly all was well. And, ten minutes later, after he had been served his martini with an olive speared on a toothpick, and he had gulped down the olive and half his martini, things even seemed rather jolly to him. Here he was, sitting with the world's most famous rug collector, *entertaining* him—and not only that, but Mr. Pope had asked Holden to "take him around."

Pope was saying something about securities he had bought. "Don't know if I trust the CEO. He may be a damned fool as far as I know. Let's go over there and ask him point blank. 'What the hell are your plans for this company?'" Holden thought that was perfectly reasonable. He and Pope would demand an answer.

"That's what I'd do," he said.

"Good. You can take me there tomorrow. And maybe you would like to help me with one other thing." It seemed as if Pope's martini had loosened his tongue, and, if Holden was seeing correctly in the dim light, Pope's face had even become flushed. As Pope talked to Holden, he looked not at him but at the waitresses who bustled about the dining room. "As you know, I am president of the International Ali Babba Society which, of course, is a rug collector's society. I would like to increase our membership here in the San Francisco Bay Area, and I'd like you to call all your friends and customers who are collectors and bring them together in Berkeley on February 30th. I'll give a talk about rugs. I'll need a slide projector and a screen." That said, Pope finished his martini and didn't seem to expect an answer. The old man waved at a bunny for another martini.

Of course Holden was happy to help Pope with his Ali Babba meeting, though he foresaw an awful lot of hassle to pull this off. He declined a second martini, knowing he would have to return to work if he got through taking Mr. Pope "around." Holden still could not shake the strangeness of sitting here with Ulysses Pope. In fact, looking at him closely—which he could do because Pope's attention was riveted on the waitresses—he had an uncanny sensation that J. Edger Hoover was sitting across from him, or possibly even Herbert Hoover. After lunch, Pope called for a third martini, and as the waitress delivered the drink and then turned away, Holden watched, horrified, as Pope pinched her bottom. The waitress whirled about and glared furiously at Holden, evidently thinking it was the youth rather than the old man who had copped the pinch. "Shame on you!" she hissed. "Just *shame!*" as if he were a bad dog. Holden's jaw dropped.

She stamped her foot once and then stomped away, never to return. Pope smiled. Neither he nor Holden said a word about the pinch. In fact, Pope seemed at ease saying nothing at all, even when the cashier, not the waitress, brought around the check and Holden said, "I'll get it." Having offered and hearing no counter offer, Holden had no choice but to follow through. He paid the bill.

Chapter Seven

"Hate to bother, lass, but I'm having
a bit of trouble, actually."

When Avery told Sarah that he despised money, he had told the truth. It sickened him to see how the common folk debased themselves for it. Once, as a young man, he had been called to appraise an estate, though it was a shabby one—the meager estate of a woman who had recently died. Her relatives wished to liquidate her Oriental rugs, and they sat teary-eyed but alert as they watched Avery inspect a sad collection of worn and dirty rugs. Kneeling, he turned the corner of a large, soiled carpet on the floor and discovered a little stash of $100 bills, perhaps six or eight of them, which the deceased must have hidden there against a rainy day—or perhaps hidden from the very same relatives who sat nearby, watching. Still on his knees, momentarily indecisive, he glanced across the room at the bereaved. It was a mistake. Before he could make a move, they were out of their seats and across the room, and they had quite unnecessarily clawed the money from his hand. Though he was sure he would have called his little discovery to their attention, each of them, after that, glared at him as if he had somehow tried to cheat them. But it was the way they glowered at each other that had most disturbed him. He could see that a horrible battle for the money was shaping up among them, and he quickly excused himself. For some time after that, Avery could not get their greedy eyes out of his mind. Really, he was sickened by the incident, and his spirit, you could say, had been bruised by the greed he had witnessed.

It was not just the money-squabbles of the lesser people that filled him with disgust. The rich, if possible, were even worse. He had been raised in a well-off family whose members constantly battled one another to become sole inheritor of their robber-baron grandfather's fortune. In their frenzy for money, his siblings, parents, aunts, uncles and cousins maneuvered and positioned and ingratiated themselves. They fawned, weaseled, lied, forged and sued. Since those days of his childhood, he had known many wealthy people whose whole focus was to inherit money and to prevent their relatives from inheriting it. But not Avery. At the age of seventeen he had simply left home, and so from that time he had had to make his own way in the world. During his youth and even now, all he wanted from life, he thought, was to remain above the noisy fray for money while yet surrounding himself with beauty.

That presented difficulties. Unfortunately, beauty frequently came at a high sticker price, and so he was often forced to scrape up some money. That proved easier for him than keeping it. Having no great fondness for the stuff, he tended to squander it, sometimes investing it badly, often giving it away and sometimes simply loosing track of it. In any case, his modus depended on giving the impression of owning it, and he became adept at making a show of having money, whether true or not. For instance, as we have seen, he found that the lines of an old Porsche 928 were just as ravishing as those of a much newer one, and furthermore, used, they cost far less than commonplace new automobiles. But, best of all, he had discovered that their front seats reclined almost fully and, during difficult times, made as comfortable a bed as any you could hope for, and their hatchbacks could store an impressive number of silk scarves, tweed hats and other personal effects for someone who often had to leave town quickly and travel light. So, even though at the moment he was inconvenienced by not having fare for a hotel room, he was able to spend the chilly, winter night after his meeting with Sarah Atwood stretched out comfortably in the fully reclined leather seat of his Porsche, parked under the stars in Berkeley's Tilden Park, a warm scarf around his neck and a wool hat to keep his head warm. Tomorrow he would sell the silk Kirman for $3000 or $300 or $50. It didn't matter. It would be enough to get him through. So now he gazed at the night sky through his moon roof and cooked up a plan.

"First read everything on the subject," he said aloud as he lay under the stars, "then come up with a design and find someone to graph it, then find a source for good wool, then someone who can spin it by hand, then a dyer and a weaver and then...have to trust myself to finish it, make it look four hundred years old." For he had been thoroughly charmed by the curator of the San Francisco Museum's rug collection, and he had decided to help her. He would *make* the rug she was looking for—the Ferrier Dragon Rug. "Sarah could waste her lifetime looking for a rug that may not exist," he thought. "Bloody waste of time. Much better for her if I cough one up. She can have just what she wants, and I'll have done her a good turn." That settled, he pulled his scarf a little tighter around his shoulders and settled in for the night.

"Money," he mumbled, already half-asleep. "It's a strange thing, but I always seem to find exactly as much of it as I need." After that, Avery lay sleeping in his bucket seat. He didn't hear the family of raccoons that came to investigate and who peered down at the sleeping man through the Porsche's moon roof on a clear, chilly night.

The famous Martin book is unusual. First, it is enormous: about two feet wide and nearly three feet high, though not at all thick—perhaps less than an inch thick. Its big, black cover is nothing more than the cover of a portfolio, and its text and illustrations are printed on huge loose leaves that are slipped inside when not in use. Sitting at a table in Berkeley's main library with the pages of Martin's old book spread before him, Avery finished reading Martin's thoughts about the Ferrier dragon rug and then turned to the back cover of its portfolio, where he found its old fashioned library card. He pulled the card from its sleeve and squinted at it. "Hah!" he laughed silently. The book had last been borrowed in 1967. "Bloody fools don't know what they have: a copy of the Martin book. Haven't even looked at it in a quarter century. Dolts! Morons! They don't deserve it." He rubbed a corner of a page between his thumb and forefinger. Its paper, yellowed with age, was heavy and textured as if handmade, and a sour odor of age rose from its pages, spread open before him on the table.

Avery experienced an impulse to rant, an almost overwhelming impulse. If he had allowed himself, he would have risen and stalked about the room and shouted into people's faces, "Fools, imbeciles! There you sit, reading your squalid little paperbacks in the library to save spending a buck at a bookstore! You are not twenty feet from a book whose beauty would change your lives, a book that could *elevate* you, a book of such quality and construction as to open your eyes forever." And more. He could have gone on forever, but a more charitable idea came to him that tempered his impulse to rant. He took a deep breath. "But why blame them for their tastes?" he thought. "They toil; they need simple pleasures—a paperback and a beer. So they leave F. R. Martin moldering on the shelf for a third of a century. They can't be blamed for what they're made of. Deane, old man," he addressed himself, "there is nothing you can do to change them." This was a familiar and comforting thought to him, and one that always led to the same conclusion. "All I can do is to redistribute the wealth from the insensate many to the caring few," and, as that thought had done so often before, it brought relief and calm to Avery as he considered how to liberate the book.

But let's be truthful. He had anticipated all this beforehand, before he had re-read Martin's familiar words and had weighed the quality of the book's paper between his thumb and forefinger. He had guessed that the book would be under-appreciated by folks of the common clay. He had foreseen even the impulse he would have to rant. And, finally, he had anticipated that, in such circumstances, his only recourse would be to pinch the book. And so he had stashed three rolls of gauze in his pants pockets and as many rolls of bandage and a neck brace.

Settled now on what he had to do, Avery gathered and straightened all the loose leaves of the Martin book and slipped them back into their oversized portfolio. He carried the book to "the stacks," the lofty racks that afforded him some privacy, and he wrapped the big book in gauze. Within three minutes the Martin book was swathed in the white surgical gauze like a mummy and nothing of its true, bookish nature was visible. Rather, it had become vaguely medical-looking. Next, he slipped a brace around his neck that held his head unnaturally high and caused him look like a victim of whiplash. And finally, seeming to struggle with the weight of his medical prop, he dragged himself to the check-out counter and interrupted a young clerk.

"Hate to bother, lass, but I'm having a bit of trouble, actually." At this he gasped as if struck by an unimaginably sharp pain. His writhing suggested that his pain must have something to do with his neck or his back. The young lady behind the counter, who had been checking out a book to a patron, looked with wide eyes at the poor man.

"Oh God! I'll call 911!"

Avery recovered from his pain just in time to stop her. "No, no dear, just a spasm. Mustn't disturb everyone. This is a library, after all." He smiled weakly. "Hush, hush and all that." But after his brave joke, he grimaced horribly, obviously weathering another spasm. The girl was at a loss as to what to do. Again she made a move for the phone.

"Ha, ha!" Avery laughed, his face pale. "It's passed. Put the phone down, dear. But if you would just help me establish traction..."

Her eyes were wide. "Establish traction?"

"Walking traction, that's what they call it. Just enough to get me out of here and into my car."

"What can I do?"

"Just strap this brace to my back."

"God, I don't know. I'll go get security!"

"No, please don't, not for me. But if you would just use this roll of tape. Rather awkward for me to do it, behind my back and all." Avery spoke through clenched teeth as if suppressing a scream from the pain. "Here," he said to her, "I'll get the tape started and then you just send it around a couple of times. Quick! Quick! I feel another spasm coming on!"

She sprinted around the counter to his side and began wrapping the tape around the "brace" and then around his trunk, silk scarf and all, around and around. The tape made a surprising amount of racket in the library as it peeled off the roll. "Nice and tight now, dear," he said. When a gentleman from Security arrived on the scene, attracted by the noise and the obvious concern of the dozens of library patrons who were watching the heroic librarian do something to the man in the neck brace, the nervous security man seemed to believe that emergency procedures were needed for a hear attack victim, and he asked Avery to lie down. "Why the devil should I do that?" Avery asked, forgetting himself for a moment.

"So I can give you artificial respiration, sir. Please lie on your back, not your stomach or I'll have to spin you over."

"Damn you, sir!" Avery shouted, his fight or flight instinct triggered by the sickening image of the man breathing in his face, or worse. It's likely that he would have fought, but by this time he was rendered nearly helpless by the wrapped-up Martin book cinched tightly to his back.

"Jack, can you tear this tape?" the young librarian asked the guard.

For the first time, Jack noticed what his colleague was doing, and he studied the situation. "Why don't you just finish off the roll?" he asked her. "That stuff's hard to tear."

Her hands had steadied. She agreed, and she wrapped the rest of the tape around Avery and his back brace. During all this Avery made such horrible, contorted faces that it occurred to the onlookers that they had just witnessed the use of some kind of emergency straightjacket on a poor fellow who had lost his mind. Nasty business.

In the end, the man from Security walked Avery to his car and tried to help him inside, but, unable to bend his back because of his brace, Avery finally had to climb head first into the back seat and *swim* his way to the driver's station. Even then, he had the devil of a time making himself comfortable in his Porsche's bucket seat.

Chapter Eight

About ten days after he had been visited by the rug gods, he arose from his desk and raised all his prices by half.

 Holden sat at his roll top desk chewing on the meaning of life. He had gone unnoticed for three years in the rug business, then wham! Ulysses Pope, the most famous rug collector in the world, appeared from nowhere and discovered him. So had Avery Deane—who *seemed* important, if Holden could only figure out who he was. But, though he had been discovered by the big boys, and though Pope had even bought a rug from him, no one else had. He was as close to bankruptcy as ever.

On the other hand, it did seem as if he had been dusted by some of the magic that trailed the famous Ulysses Pope. In trying to put together a meeting of local collectors so Pope could enlist them for his Ali Babba Society, Holden had called everyone on his customer-list plus all the collectors he knew who bought their rugs elsewhere. They had all been surprised to hear that Holden had some association with Ulysses Pope. About a week later, Holden's phone had begun to ring. Some were just calling to confirm that they would be at the meeting, but others wanted Holden's advice about this and that. "Hey Holden," a collector named Griff Norton asked him, "you know that Caucasian rug I bought at auction lately? You know the one I mean?"

"Yes, I do," he said. Holden had been there. He had watched the collector buy a rug and pay good money for it— too much money—when he knew Griff could have bought a better rug for far less money in his own store.

"Well, what do you think it is? I mean, I can't really decide."

"Really? Isn't it a Shirvan? With those cotton selvages? Cotton wefts. That's what it looks like, too. It's a Shirvan. What else could it be?"

"Uh, well of course that was my thought, too. What else could it be?"

"Right."

"Hey Holden, what's this I hear about you showing Ulysses Pope around?"

"Yeah."

"Really?"

"Yeah."

"Cool."

Phone calls like that. Suddenly rug dealers and collectors wanted his professional advice and some wanted to get themselves invited to Pope's meeting. Holden, as he had already noted, had been invisible for the past three years in business. Now everyone was calling him up. But they weren't buying his rugs.

About ten days after he had been visited by the rug gods Pope and Deane, he arose from his desk and raised all his prices by half. It went against his grain, but, he told himself, "What do I have to lose?" Then he had an anxiety attack and actually had to go out to the sidewalk and pace as fast as he could in front of his store, and pant like a dog. His breath turned to steam in the cold February air. But he got so worried that he might be missing an important phone call that he had to return to his showroom, where he continued his rapid pacing and rabid breathing.

A lonely week later, during which many people phoned but no customers walked through the door, Avery Deane breezed in. So did Griff Norton, just moments later. Griff collected Caucasian rugs and he popped in about once every three months and never bought anything. Instead, he always described to Holden in excruciating detail the rugs he had bought from other dealers, dwelling especially on minute details of their borders. Holden was always terribly glad for him, congratulating him on his good fortune. This time when Griff walked through the door, Avery Deane went right to him and shook his hand.

"Pleased to meet you," he said. "My name is Avery Deane. Turkish rugs, am I right? You collect Turkish rugs."

"Caucasian."

Avery suddenly pulled his hand back and seemed uncomfortable. Then he cheered up. "Well, lucky I got here first."

"Why?" Griff was puzzled and seemed annoyed.

"Ha! You dog. You thought you'd buy Holden's Kuba before I could get a crack at it, but I got here first!"

"What Kuba?"

Avery looked surprised. Then the light seemed to dawn on him. "Right," he said, "what Kuba? Lot's of good rugs here. Why focus on the Kuba? Did you see Holden's Marasali Shirvan? Or the Karabaugh?" Avery began trying to call

Griff's attention to a Karabaugh mounted on the rear wall, but Griff ignored him and began a quick prowl through the showroom, searching. "Or this Kazak?" Avery called to him from across the room. "Did you see this Karachopf Kazak?" But Griff didn't even glance his way.

Holden looked from Avery to Griff, from Griff to Avery. He watched as Griff stopped before a late 19th century Zeykhur Kuba with an ivory field and two medallions that looked like galaxies radiating in bursts of energy. Griff peered at it as though he had never seen it before, though Holden knew that he had often walked past it with indifference. When Griff examined the rug's price tag, Holden had to look away. He had just raised the price from $2000 to $3000.

From the other side of the room where Holden now couldn't see him, Avery Deane shouted, "Holden, I do have first crack at that Kuba, don't I? $4,000, right?"

Holden didn't know what to say. If Deane had wanted to buy his Kuba why hadn't he done it before? Anyway, it was a magnificent rug. He had never before realized just how good a rug it was. Its "running dog" border was full of graceful motion. Finally he responded, awkwardly. "It's $3000 and I guess it's whoever wants to buy it."

"I do," Griff said. "Sold."

"You do? You want to buy it?" Holden couldn't help sounding surprised.

"I do."

"What? What did you say?" Deane shouted.

"Uh, Griff just bought it, Mr. Deane." Deane didn't answer, but in a moment he appeared.

"Beg pardon, Holden?"

"Griff just bought it."

"The Kuba?"

Griff faced him and said, "Yes."

"But that's impossible. It was for sale just a moment ago, before you came in."

"Well, it's not for sale now," Griff said. "Maybe you should have been a little more decisive." Griff smiled at Deane, not kindly. Deane began to protest, then he seemed to wilt, and he slunk out of sight as Griff wrote a check and Holden accepted it and wrote a receipt. A few minutes later, Griff Norton walked out the door, a rolled Kuba under his arm. When he was gone, Avery Deane seemed perfectly happy. Holden was surprised. He had thought the small man with the wonderful voice would be disappointed.

Chapter Nine

"Perhaps the gentleman would be more comfortable
looking at shiny new rugs?"

Holden's Kuba—it was now *Griff's* Kuba—was
born in the northern foothills of the Greater
Caucasus Mountains, in Zeykhur, a village that
lies along a river near the Caspian Sea. Most of
Zeykhur's villagers were native people known as Lesghis,
renowned for weaving rugs of two distinctive designs. One,
not often seen, was based on realistic looking flowers that
seemed strangely European. In fact the flowers—the way
they were drawn—*were* European. They were French
flowers, woven in the 19th and early 20th centuries for
Russian intelligentsia in love with all things French. But
there was another design for which Zeykhur was famous, and
this was the design of Holden's Kuba. Known by the world
simply as Zeykhur, the design has two or more medallions
that look like the colorful snowflakes in a child's
kaleidoscope. Each seems to have exploded from its center
and to have hurled arms of energy and color out into the
universe of its field.

By 1880, when Silamova Breshev wove Holden's rug, she
and her fellow villagers had forgotten the origins of the
Zeykhur design. (Unknown to them, it was a simplified and,
some might say, a corrupted element from the famous

dragon rugs woven in the Caucasus a hundred and two hundred years earlier, which, in turn, were most likely based on even earlier dragon rugs from China, such as the Ferrier Dragon Rug, and were, some might say, corruptions of them.) Silamova didn't care much about where the design came from. In fact, the merchant who commissioned her to weave the rug called it "design twelve," and that's how she thought of it, too.

But if she had no deep curiosity about the antecedents of design twelve, she was not indifferent to the quality of her work. Not at all. Now 39, she had woven 26 complete rugs and, as a learner, had worked on others with her mother. She was at the top of her powers. So when she began to weave Holden's rug, she had a picture in her mind of how her rug should look when it was finished. Some of her friends were experimenting with the new dyes that came in cans and were cheap and easy to use, but she had her doubts about them. She loved bright, happy colors as much as her friends did, but these colors from cans seemed to her bright almost to a fault. When she imagined the rug she was about to weave, she pictured it in the deeper, darker shades of red, green, blue, yellow and rose that she could extract from the dyes she had known all her life. And so she chose the harder road of extracting natural dyes from plants near the village.

Silamova had reached that stage in her craft in which she was unconscious of her hands as they wove. Like a musician, she worked within a rigid form—design number twelve—yet managed to express herself within it through grace notes of weaving, whimsies of color-choice, and by improvising when the spirit struck her.

And then one day she tied the last knot and her rug was completed. She pampered it for a while, clipping imaginary loose ends like a barber unwilling to say *fini*, and patted and straightened it when she walked by. And finally there came a day when she gave it to her husband to sell. It was gone. She never again thought of Holden's rug in particular, nor did it ever occur to her that she should have kept it. But her rug-weaving was a source of pleasure and income throughout her long life.

Silamova's rug quickly made its way up the mercantile ladder from her village to the district's rug center, Kuba, from where it was sold to a dealer in Moscow. It is a strange fact that rug dealers love rugs. It is rare for a dealer to be indifferent to a charming rug. Even helpers who toss them into stacks or sweep them recognize and love special rugs. Dealers often take home their favorites, even when they really can't afford to. Their mates berate them and insist that they return the rug to their businesses to be turned into money for a modern bathroom or a kitchen re-model, and so the rugs go back into inventory and a homemaker or collector eventually becomes its owner. So it was with Silamova's rug. Every dealer who put his hands on it wanted to keep it, and some did for a time. They all recognized that it was different from run-of-the-mill rugs. It was gorgeous.

"Oh my God," the wife said. She wrapped a forearm low across her abdomen. Her husband noticed and wondered about it. Something visceral had happened to her, more sexual than spiritual, he thought. "I want it," she said. The husband experienced a twinge of jealousy. The rug dealer noticed her unconscious self-embrace, too, of course, and thought he had a sale. He did. Ludmila Badilova and her husband Pierre took the Kuba home with them that afternoon and became its first real owners.

Pierre and Ludmila were members of Moscow's rising bourgeoisie. Pierre had developed an inexpensive way of galvanizing lead pipe at a time (the waning years of the 19th century) when indoor plumbing was becoming widespread in the cities. When he and his wife bought the Kuba, they already occupied the estate in which they believed they would spend the rest of their lives, a wonderful house and thirty forested acres close to the Moscow city limits. Later, after all the troubles began with the Bolsheviks, they came to regret that it was not somewhat more removed from the city. In 1913, the Bolsheviks seized Ludmila's and Pierre's mansion, their land and all their possessions, including Silamova's Kuba. But, during the twenty years that Pierre and Ludmila owned the Kuba, Ludmila, especially, was devoted to it. It lay at the foot of a staircase, and each time she descended the stairs, at least several time a day, the glowing little rug infused her with a little burst of joy, which she felt quite palpably in some abdominal organ or another. And then it was gone, seized along with everything else, and the two were lucky even to be alive and living in a one-bedroom apartment in Moscow.

For a time, the mansion served the Bolsheviks as a regional administrative center. Its furniture remained in place, including its rugs and carpets. But rather than admiring the rugs and art and furniture, the Bolsheviks barely tolerated them, for to them they represented the self-indulgent excesses of the bourgeoisie. Eventually, after the crushing years following World War I, the Bolsheviks rounded up hundreds of thousands of Caucasian and Turkmen rugs from the old estates and exported them to raise money for the struggling new Soviet economy.

Under the cover of moonless nights, Henry Garemejian was spirited out of his Turkish village and then out of Turkey by relatives after both his parents were murdered there during the persecution of Armenians in 1911. As a young adult in 1930, he began a long career in the rug business in San Francisco by importing Caucasian rugs that, at that time, were pouring out of the Soviet Union. A family member in Armenia sent him a consignment of 200 Caucasian rugs and told him to pay for them as they sold. They cost Henry an average of $23 and he sold them for $35.

At that time and until well into the sixties, all the heavy, rather course rugs from the Southern Caucasus were known in American rug circles as *Kazaks* (even though there was no people or village by that name), and the finer, thinner rugs from the north, including Kubas, were called *Cabistans* (even though there was no such place or people). One of the Cabistans that came into Henry's possession in that first shipment from Armenia was Ludmila's Kuba. Now 34 years old and still in good condition, it had bloomed with the luster that rugs blessed with good wool and good dyes acquire from reasonable use on the floor—these were the years before everyone came to wear rubber-soled tennis shoes indoors— and its colors had softened nicely from use and time. Very soon Henry Garemejian sold it and 24 others to an upscale San Francisco department store, W.J. Sloan's. Sloan's rug buyer, also an Armenian, recognized that the Cabistan was special and he priced it at $135 rather than the $110 he charged for the others. Nonetheless, it quickly sold to a doctor from a wealthy suburb of San Francisco called Hillsborough.

Men often are left cold by the fine linen, silverware, crystal, lace and other household notions that drive their wives nearly crazy with acquisitiveness. Yet many men are charmed to pieces by Oriental rugs. They feel they can sink their teeth into a good rug. There is no accounting for it.

Dr. Chase was one such man. His very first acquisition, the Kuba, was like the birth of an unplanned baby. It was a love child. He stumbled upon it in the rug department at Sloan's while his wife was shopping for feather pillows upstairs. He was fooling around, killing time. He turned the corners of a few rugs in stacks and looked at the price tags of rugs on the walls. He checked the time on his wristwatch. With one wingtip shoe he turned the corner of a carpet on the floor. He stooped lower to flip through a stack of smaller pieces that reminded him of Navajo rugs. He felt that these were more his style. Blessedly no salesman approached him and he took his time looking at these rugs since he had at least another half hour to kill. Some had flaws and that surprised him: designs that seemed cut off or, at least, unfinished; stripes of color that changed unexpectedly; and some were even a little worn. Yet they were expensive. One was more expensive than the others. That was annoying. He liked it especially, he thought. From the half he could see, it seemed...not-Western. It seemed not-anything: not European, not Oriental, and (on closer examination) not Navajo. It was unlike Islamic tile, Greek art, or Grandma Moses.

"Can I help you, sir?"

"Blast," Dr. Chase swore silently. But still, maybe he did need help. "Well, perhaps you could let me see this rug a little better?"

"Of course, sir." The salesman was in a well-tailored suit and Dr. Chase thought he had a bit of a superior attitude. Effortlessly the salesman exposed the Kuba and he held it for Dr. Chase to admire, letting its bottom third lie on the wooden showroom floor and holding the rest in the air so that it caught a beam from a spotlight, just so. "This is a Cabistan, sir, one of our finest." Dr. Chase struggled to think of the right questions to ask but found nothing to say. The salesman was not bothered at all. "This rug," he said, "was the work of a young bride and it was woven as part of her dowry. That is evident in the care she took in its weaving." He was warming up. "You see how finely it is woven, sir?" With a deft move he flipped over one of the rug's corners, exposing its back without even having to kneel to do so. The doctor stared at the rug's back for a moment but had no idea what he was looking at. He supposed it looked pretty fine.

Finally he thought of something to say, something appropriately skeptical. "Is this rug in good condition? It looks tattered there along the edge."

Evidently this was the wrong thing to say, because the fellow in the expensive suit frowned slightly and explained with strained patience, "Sir, this is a very old rug, an antique, sir. A certain evidence of use is appropriate. But perhaps the gentleman would be more comfortable looking at shiny new rugs?"

Dr. Chase thought he detected a patronizing tone and refused to let himself be led to a stack of "shiny new rugs." Instead he asked, "How old is this one?"

"1846, sir, give or take a year or two," he answered without hesitation.

"Eighty four years old?" Dr. Chase was sorry he had let his amazement show, like a rube. The salesman nodded complacently, evidently in a better mood now. "Uh, how can you tell that it was woven for a dowry?"

"Sir, can you see that the selvages are wrapped in blue thread?" Of course he could. "And do you notice that each end is finished in blue?" Certainly. "That, sir, is an ancient tradition in the Caucasus: Blue ends and edges, the sign of a dowry piece."

Dr. Chase was secretly considering buying the rug, but the thought put him in some confusion. What would his wife say, she who dictated all that went into the house? He considered going to find her but he thought that might seem weak. In the meantime, the fellow was explaining something about the border of the rug, something about the tortoise and the hare, but he was barely listening. "After all," the doctor asked himself, "why do I work from sunup to sundown? I have the money. What good is life without a little joy?" The salesman now addressed the center of the rug, the *field*, he called it. Something about a sun-god. "Maybe she'll like it," the doctor speculated.

Surprisingly, she did, though she would not let him put it in the library where he thought it would look good. She was firm about it going into a guest bedroom. He used to visit it there and sit on the edge of the bed with books he bought about Oriental rugs, comparing his rug to pictures in books. From what he could tell from the books, the salesman had got it just right, though some writers thought the border was about dogs running rather than hares racing tortoises. This was the beginning of Dr. Chase's fifty-year love affair with Oriental rugs, and when finally he sloughed off his mortal coil, his Kuba really was 84 years old.

In 1980 Dr. Chase's estate was consigned to auction and a Berkeley antiques dealer named Al, with an eye for Oriental rugs, bought the Kuba. He was the first since the rug had left the old country to identify it as a Zeykhur, though at that time the word was commonly pronounced it *Seyjour*. It never saw the inside of his shop but rather it went home with him and became an honored part of his collection. In 1999 Al was unable to pay his payroll tax and, under duress, he sold the Zeykhur for $1500 to avoid being shut down.

Our friend Holden bought it and hung it on the wall of his new rug store and fiercely admired the rug until it had hung there so long and had been passed over by so many collectors that he nearly ceased to see it. Then Avery Deane told him he was "giving it away" and had suggested loudly that he "lock it up." That was when Holden raised the price and sold it to Griff. Or was it Avery who had done the selling? He wondered.

Chapter Ten

Of course Sarah's business instincts had proven sound.

After Sarah made her debut as a rug expert at the Carpet Museum's show and tell, her rise to stardom in the rug world had been spectacular. In fact, even at that first show-and-tell she had made a deep impression on people, particularly on men between the ages of fourteen and ninety. For instance, as she extolled the quality of her Belouch prayer rug's soft wool, she playfully roughed up its fleecy wool and then fondled and smoothed it in a way that upset them all. When she asked if any "gentleman" was willing to hold up her rug so that the audience could see it better, there were so many volunteers and they were so insistent on helping her that she had to settle the matter by holding it up herself.

Of course Sarah's business instincts had proven sound. Her decision to print Charles Francis Green's name on her business cards had opened doors. Opportunities had arisen. And she had never had to explain to Green why his name was there, in bold letters. Either he hadn't found out or he was too much a gentleman to confront a lady. Often she called on Green to help her with rug matters. She would show him photographs of antique rugs that clients wished to sell or rugs they wished to purchase and he would graciously identify and appraise them. Each time she would thank him for his cooperation.

While she pursued her increasingly successful consultation business, she undertook training in the docent program at the National Carpet Museum. After she became a qualified docent, Sarah added "National Carpet Museum" to her business card and then dropped out of the program without ever having had to guide tiresome museum-visitors. In the meantime she had begun taking graduate classes at Georgetown University in "Textile Arts." Fortunately, her professors understood that her duties at the Carpet Museum, which she may have exaggerated somewhat, often prevented her from attending classes and adversely affected her performance on occasional exams, and they took that in to account as they graded her work. In record time she was able to add "Masters, Textile Arts" to her business card. So now it looked like this:

Sarah Atwood MA, Textile Arts
Oriental Rugs and Carpets
National Carpet Museum, Washington, D.C.
In Cooperation with Mr. Charles Francis Green

As her career prospered, Sarah never doubted that she had chosen the right one, even though she knew that success meant having to walk among her clients and colleagues disguised as something she was not. It was not her ignorance of rugs that she had to mask—that was hardly a problem at all—but her *dislike* for Oriental rugs. Working with Oriental rugs nearly every day, she had quickly become so sick of them that she could have vomited. But really, she had never cared for them. Of course there was her Serapi with which she had at least felt herself to be on friendly terms, but even this feeling had dimmed. Not only that, but after working and socializing with collectors, dealers, curators, importers, decorators, homeowners, writers and scholars and even a few weavers, it was her conviction that every last one of them, like her, was faking their enthusiasm for rugs, each for their own reasons but mainly for money. That and attention. Collectors and homeowners craved attention; the others craved money.

In a feisty mood once, she had prodded the National Carpet Museum's director, Kyle Berman, to see whether she could penetrate *his* disguise. At that time Sarah was in the docent program and Berman was her boss. One afternoon, someone from the public brought a rug to the museum to find out what it was, how old it was and what it was worth. The Carpet Museum never got involved in appraising rugs, but often someone on the staff found time to inform people about what they had. It so happened that Kyle and Sarah had been the ones to whom the job fell, and of course they were able to tell the fellow all about his rug. It was a south Persian gabbeh, circa maybe 1920, the kind of rug that a tribal people (the Qashgayi) wove near Shiraz, usually, at that time, for personal use rather than export. This gabbeh was dominated by a tiger that filled the entire field. It was a ridiculous tiger, really, woven in the most lurid synthetic dyes of edgy orange, flaming pink and fire engine red—not the kind of thing the Carpet Museum would have kept in its collection. Yet Kyle was nearly poetic in its praise.

77

"It is a wonderful survivor," he told its owner, "of a long Persian tradition of bringing lions and tigers to life in their rugs. It is possible that even in the 20s, when this rug was woven, weavers no longer remembered the why and wherefore of their lions and tigers, but they owe their tradition to the days of Darius the Great, whose personal symbol was a lion holding a sword." And more. After a quarter of an hour, the rug's owner left, elated.

When the fellow was gone, Sarah smiled. "Well done, Kyle. There's a happy customer. Maybe he will someday feel inclined to donate money to the museum."

"Well, he had a fun rug."

"Fun? I'd say it was nice of you not to make fun of it." Sarah said "nice," but she thought the real answer was that Kyle had been smart to forebear telling the rug's owner what he really thought.

But he played dumb. "Make fun of it? Why would I do that?"

She laughed. For a moment Sarah tried to imagine living in the same house with the gabbeh and its lurid colors and its comic book tiger. She couldn't, but then there weren't many rugs she wanted to be in the same house with after working hours. "Well, let's just say that you would make a good politician."

"Thank you Sarah," he said, a little stiffly, "but I liked that rug. It really is from a great tradition, you know." Sarah took a breath to argue with him but stopped. He really wasn't going to step out of his disguise, even with her. He was the director of the Carpet Museum, and he hadn't got there by indulging himself, she thought. He was going to keep his feelings to himself. For the first time Sarah admired Kyle

Berman. He was disciplined and that is why he had risen to the top. His success was no accident. She felt blessed to have absorbed this lesson early in her career. Never let down the front. It didn't occur to her that he actually may have liked the rug.

Her career did seem blessed. As soon as she had added her new Master's Degree to her resume, she had begun sending it to museums around the country along with a letter inquiring about positions as curator of rug and textile departments. She always included a professionally produced photograph of herself in her package. In the photo she was proudly holding a rug, of course, but it was she who dominated the photo and not the rug. Her resume got nibbles. Then she got a bite. She was invited to curate the rug and textile division of the San Francisco Museum. Just like that. When she showed up to take the reins, those who had hired her wanted to know all the latest about her famous mentor, Charles Francis Green.

After being on the job for a year or so, she met with a strange fellow with a beautiful voice, Avery Deane. The next day, Sarah phoned Ulysses Pope. "I couldn't pin him down, Ulysses. He said the rug was still in China and hinted that it would have to be smuggled out." She was one of the very few people in rug circles who had the nerve to call Pope by his first name.

"Has he seen it himself?"

"My impression is that he hasn't."

"So it could all be smoke and mirrors. What did he want?"

"He asked how much the museum is willing to pay for it."

"And what did you tell him?"

"He had heard it said in Europe and New York that the San Francisco Museum was ready to pay a million dollars for it. I told him that it was not the museum but a private collector who was interested and that his figure was approximately correct. Then I cut the conversation short, saying that I wasn't interested in talking about hypotheticals. I told him to bring me the rug when he had it."

"Good. He may just be on a fishing expedition. Still, if he's got something, I want you to land it. Don't forget that there's money in it for you."

"Which, because of my position here, we needn't mention again."

"No need to. Just land that rug."

Off the phone now, Sarah thought again about what Avery Deane had said. "You're just like me, my dear. If there's anything people such as us—true lovers of the arts—if there's anything we despise, it's money. We won't even talk about it." A true lover of the arts? No, she was someone who had merely put on the trappings of one. Despise money? She laughed. We won't even talk about money? That was the only thing he had got right. Especially we won't talk about a $100,000 commission if she could put the Ferrier Dragon Rug in Pope's hands. And certainly we won't talk about it where someone from the Museum might hear of it, because museums frown on their curators setting up little side deals. And maybe we won't talk about it at all when, somehow, some way, she might manage to put the whole million dollars in her purse. Or suitcase. Because she wasn't fooling around in a museum for the rest of her life.

Chapter Eleven

He made old rugs for the joy of creating,
and, besides, he loved old rugs.

 Avery spoke to Sarah in his deep, rich voice as he began to create his Ching Dynasty dragon rug. "*Create*, my dear. Not re-produce, and certainly not fake. Together we will make a rug that has never before existed, so how can it be a copy or a fake?" As he imagined talking to Sarah—that is, imagined in the sense that children sometimes imagine playmates, and not at all in the sense of hallucinating—he gazed at a blank white page in a large drawing tablet and held a pencil in his right hand. Avery had studied the Martin book and read every word ever written about the Ferrier Dragon Rug, and now he was ready to give it life. "I'm doing this for you, Sarah. To make you happy."

He had done "this" before. In fact it could be said that making antique rugs was what he *did*. Oh, of course, he bought and sold the occasional vintage automobile or antique bronze statuette. He bought and sold nearly anything, really, to hustle up money. But his calling was fashioning antique Oriental rugs. And, just as artists who work in oils or acrylic are happy to say they have their works in famous galleries and museums, Deane could have bragged that his work was represented in some of the best private and institutional collections of Oriental rugs in the world—except that he had to keep quiet about it because the collectors and museums which owned his works believed them to be at least a hundred years old.

Once, in his youth, he had heard a rug dealer joke, "They aren't making old rugs any more." That thought had deeply disturbed him and it continued to rattle around in his head. Later it occurred to him that maybe someone *should* be making old rugs. Otherwise, soon enough they would all be worn out and gone. So he had given it a try. In his first effort he had used store-bought, machine-spun wool and had woven the rug himself. When it was finished, he clipped its pile short like an old rug's and consigned it to auction. The auctioneer, at least, was fooled, and he offered it as an "old Hamadan." Apparently at least one other person took it to be old, and it sold. From that time, antique rugs were Deane's medium.

He made old rugs for the joy of creating. He wove them to challenge himself. But, more, he wove them for the delicious secret knowledge they gave him—knowledge that confirmed his poor opinion of the wealthy people who believed they were collecting *works of art*. Having fooled them with his rugs, he knew them to be fools. "Idiots, morons, dolts!" he called the smug museum curators and directors who collected *works of art* for the amusement of the wealthy. "I know something you don't: that your expertise is a sham; that your money is thrown away; that your *works of art* are mirages."

He took special delight in dreaming up and creating rugs so *hip* that wealthy collectors simply couldn't resist them. There were only eight known star Kazaks in the world? He made the ninth and arranged to have it discovered at auction. It was the absolutely coolest star Kazak of them all. Within its classic star design, he planted tiny animals that some believed to be antelope and others thought to be dogs. He designed elements that a famous rug scholar claimed to represent earth goddesses. Critics argued. A human face peered out from the very center of the centermost star. And finally, the background color of its major border was a rare shade of pistachio green that was absolutely irresistible to collectors. Rug dealers and agents from museums swarmed to the obscure auction gallery outside of London to vie for it. All agreed that the rug was well worth the $120,000 the National Carpet Museum, in the end, paid for it at auction.

The other rug he produced at about the same time, the Arabachi, was just as hip. Why? Because of an absolutely insignificant technical anomaly involving the rug's construction. Instead of the usual Z-spin and S-ply of a Turkmen rug's foundation, this one was S-spun and Z-plied. It was thought to be from a previously unknown group of rugs. No one considered that it might simply be the work of a dyslexic weaver—or, of course, that it might be a hoax. If not for its anomaly, the rug would have been worth four or five thousand dollars. Though it was not an attractive rug, the National Carpet Museum bought it at the same auction for $90,000.

Avery Deane took a fine pleasure knowing that some of the world's rug experts were monkeys, but his deepest satisfaction was from anticipating that someday his rugs would be discovered to be fakes, thus ensuring that their owners would have to acknowledge that they were idiots. To ensure that this moment would come, he wove into each of his creations a clue. For instance, he worked two dozen knots into the star Kazak that he had colored with a dye not invented until two decades after the rug had supposedly been woven. Sooner or later, he knew, someone would subject the dyes to modern analysis and the cat would be out of the bag.

Of course he also made antique rugs for money. But somehow he never managed to hang onto it. Of the $210,000 the rugs had sold for to the National Rug Museum, Deane saw only $150,000 after the auction gallery's commission, and that went to get him out of a scrape he was in at the time. The money was nice, but...no, that wasn't it. The pleasure for him was the satisfaction of a job well done.

Now he began to pencil in the outlines of Sarah's rug, a simple rectangle and then a smaller rectangle within. Already two spaces were defined: border and field. Then, the dragon: Deane placed him to one side of the field, facing forward, and gave him menacing teeth and a long, drooping and finally up-curling mustache and a bristling beard. "Eyes," he said aloud, and quickly he sketched eyes that glowered so fiercely they seemed almost comic. Then the dragon's sinuous, scaly trunk and tail and his four legs, on each of which was a five-toed claw. All along his back ran saw-toothed armor like the sharp dorsal fins of a shark.

"Who is this dragon?" he mused, studying what he had drawn. "What sort of beast have we created, Sarah? A fierce and fearsome dragon, yes, but one so menacing that he delights us. Does he keep us from a treasure? Frighten us away? Or does he *protect* us with the fire he breathes? Hah! That's it! He guards *us*, keeps *us* safe from harm! My kind of dragon, Sarah, my kind of dragon. Supreme deity in the heavens and supreme protector on earth, our emperor. Let us bow our heads."

Avery began sketching again, drawing sideways-facing dragons in each corner. "And because he rules the waters, we will border him with waves." The artist penciled Chinese waves along each edge, surveyed what he had drawn and finally crooned, "Enough, enough, enough."

Now to color. This, too, he had thought about. "We'll lay our imperial dragon on an imperial yellow background, Sarah. I'm sure he would approve." Exchanging his black lead pencil for a brush, he squeezed yellow watercolor onto a pallet, diluted it with water, added a spot of red and then brushed it on the pebbled paper around the five dragons. When it dried, he topped it with a thin glaze of red and brown. "Imperial yellow to frame our dragon, love. What else?" And then the dragon. He painted first in blues, three shades, then white for the dragon's scales and for his teeth, beard and mustache. Finished with the central dragon, he painted the corner dragons and then, finally, the water waves that formed the border. And having reached the moment to stop, he stopped, a challenge for any artist!

He stood back to view his work. "I think you'll be pleased, Sarah. I believe you will."

The Ferrier Dragon rug had already cost Deane his Porsche. He had sold it—as he had sacrificed his various Porsches so often in the past—for what he needed at the moment. This time it was the shelter and materials and labor to create a 350-year-old rug. The shelter, a studio apartment on the north end of Berkeley's Shattuck Avenue, had not come cheaply, and he wasn't sure he had money left to buy the wool and pay a dyer and a weaver. But Deane had an unshakable faith that, chips down, he would have exactly the amount of money he needed. Money *came* to him, he believed, and so he never worried about it.

He had drafted the rug's design and had chosen its colors. Now it was time to find help. Though he had drafted and woven and clipped his first several works himself, over the years he had learned to leave the technical work of rug-making to experts. That was especially true for this rug. For one thing, it would have to be woven with an asymmetrical knot, as nearly all Chinese rugs are, and he specialized in tying the other kind: the symmetrical knot. Secondly, he knew that this rug, for which someone apparently was ready to spend a million dollars, would be examined very carefully and that its dyes were likely to be subjected to chemical analysis and would have to be made from natural substances. And finally, it would have to be made from hand-spun wool rather than off-the-shelf machine-spun wool. So he needed a weaver, a dyer and a spinner. In addition, he needed someone able to put each individual colored knot into its own square on a piece of graph paper so that a weaver could use it as a map from which to weave the rug. Where in northern California could he find such people? He guessed: Little Kabul.

Little Kabul was so named by the large Afghan population living in Fremont, California, about 25 miles south of Oakland. Over 30,000 of them had been attracted to Fremont by its Kabul-like climate and by the California coastal range of mountains nearby that reminded them of the Halvand Mountains outside Kabul. "Among   30,000 Afghans, surely," he reasoned, "I can find one who can graph a rug design and others who can spin, dye and weave. But I can't very well walk to Little Kabul, can I Sarah? I'll need a ride. I believe I'll call on my friend, Holden." For he had purposely found an apartment within walking distance of his rug store.

Chapter Twelve

He even sniffed the rugs.
Something was wrong, but what?

 As Avery Deane was in his new digs in Berkeley inventing the Ferrier dragon rug, just five miles away at the University of California, Marley Phillips III conducted a seminar for archeology students entitled Uncovering Archeological Fakes. It was an art that had already made him famous in some circles, and the seminar was well attended. "Some artifacts just don't *smell* right," he began, and his students were immediately enthralled. One wrote down "smell" in her notebook.

He was thinking about the two rugs in the Carpet Museum's collection that had never felt quite right to him: the so-called Ninth Star Kazak and the Arabachi. For years, each time the Museum displayed them, he had peered closely at them, disturbed. When museum guards weren't present, he turned the corners of these rugs and snuck looks at their backs. He bent back their pile from the front and examined their knots. He ran his hand over their wool pile and, yes, even sniffed at the rugs. *Something* was wrong, but what?

Kyle Berman, director of the museum, wouldn't let Marley have a real go at them, not even a little snip or two from their pile so he could analyze their dyes. So one day Phillips had smuggled a tiny pair of cuticle scissors into the museum and he did a little snipping when no one was looking. Later, in his laboratory, he had analyzed the rugs' dyes and had concluded that, beyond any doubt at all, the two rugs were outright fakes. Spectrometric analysis showed the dyes to be Swiss formulations of a modern chromium type, and one of the dyes had been introduced just 20 years earlier. The rugs were essentially brand new, no question. And yet, he couldn't blow the whistle on them without admitting to having diminished the two rugs by a few grams each, which, fakes or not, one just doesn't do without permission. Phillips had to keep his lip zipped, and that proved difficult. Possessed of information that would have shown him to be a smart fellow, he was tempted to share it.

On the other hand, there was nothing to stop him from learning what he could about the forger of the rugs—for he had no doubt that one person or group had made both of them: Their wool and dyes were identical. He had begun his investigation by looking through the 1989 auction catalogue in which the rugs were advertised. Both were said to be "The Property of a Gentleman." Phillips knew that such an attribution was common when a seller wished to remain anonymous, and he wasn't surprised when the auction gallery near London that had sold the rugs absolutely refused to yield any information about the person or persons who had consigned the rugs. That seemed like the end of the trail. However, with the instincts of an archeologist, he decided to dig a little deeper.

Phillips began by interviewing New York City rug dealers who specialized in antique rugs. He knew many of them, and many knew him by reputation, for he had done much to debunk the Earth Goddess craze that had swept the rug world in the late 1980s. Some regarded him as a spoiler, since interpreting various geometric designs as "Earth Goddesses" had inflamed the imaginations of rug collectors all around the world for a time and had been good for business. Still, dealers were flattered that he asked them for advice.

After friendly chit-chat, he would ask them, "Who can you think of that would be capable of forging 19th century Caucasian and Turkmen rugs? Unfortunately, I'm not at liberty to divulge which particular rugs this person may have faked. But, when you think of all your customers and colleagues and contacts, who among them might be smart enough and well-enough informed and dishonest enough to fake old rugs?" Strangely, without exception, the rug dealers' first reaction was to smile. They were intrigued. But most of them quickly saw where this was leading and became at least a little balky.

"Does that mean that you're going to start a big stink about forged rugs? Get collectors all stirred up and afraid to buy a rug because it might be a fake?"

"Not at all," he would reply. "It means that I would like to stop rug forgery before it becomes a problem. I believe there is only one person faking rugs today, and if we can put him out of business, we'll do the industry a big favor."

"I don't know, maybe the best thing is to leave well enough alone." That's how most of them answered. And yet, they *were* intrigued, and most of them began to speculate. They dismissed most of their collectors as being far from sophisticated enough to fake an old rug. But several of them mentioned a "picker" named Pierre. "He's smart enough," they said, "and devious enough." No one knew his last name but all said that he wandered from one antique-rug shop to another and could readily be recognized by his signature snakeskin vest.

"What?"

"Snakeskin vest. He wears it all the time."

"Hm. Pierre. Is he French?"

"I don't know what the guy is, but I don't think he's French. He's just a guy who wears a snakeskin vest. He could be your man though, a crazy guy like that. But listen, don't publicize this, okay? Let's keep this stuff about fake antique rugs within the rug community, all right?"

"That's just what I would like to do," Phillips said, ambiguously.

Other dealers spoke of a man with an accent. An English accent, they thought, or maybe not quite English. British Empire, anyway: maybe Canadian or Australian or South African or something. "He knows his stuff," one dealer told him, "like knots and how many wefts between rows of knots and spin and ply and all that."

"But why do you mention him in particular?"

"I don't know. Because he's just kind of a mysterious figure, I guess. I don't think anyone knows where he's from or exactly who he is or whether he's a rug dealer or a collector or what. I don't even know his name. Small man with a big voice, and I mean really big voice. A beautiful voice, really. A pretty slippery fellow, if you ask me. He might be your man."

Several people mentioned him. One rug dealer said he would phone Phillips if the fellow ever showed up in New York again. That was something, at least.

Phillips ran into Pierre. Of course there was no mistaking his snakeskin vest. "Is your name Pierre," he asked him?

"Who wants to know?" Pierre snarled.

"Oh, sorry. I'm Marley Phillips. I've heard that you really know your stuff about Oriental rugs."

"Fuck off."

Phillips did. He had lost interest in Pierre, maybe because his vest was so ratty looking. His whole act was ratty. Marley Phillips believed that whoever made the star Kazak and the Arabachi would be classier. He didn't want Pierre to be his adversary. He wanted better.

So as Phillips guided the graduate archeology students through the techniques and science of ferreting out fakes, through carbon dating and spectrometry, he thought back to the mystery man with the beautiful voice. "Now there's an adversary," he thought. "But no name and no country, just an accent. Well, sooner or later I'll get him."

Chapter Thirteen

"It's a Bijar, man." His voice rising now, "A Bijar, Tom. Not a sniveling little Chevy, man, but a Bently! A Rolls! "

Holden was happy to see Deane pop through the door of his shop. "Maybe he has the silk Kirman," he thought. A week earlier, Deane had asked him if he would like to buy into a rug that he had found at auction in London. Deane told him that he had successfully bid for the rug but hadn't yet paid for it. If Holden wanted to, he was welcome to split the cost of the rug and own it jointly. A silk Kirman? That was a rug so rare that, frankly, Holden had never heard of one. He was inclined to be careful, though. First of all, he would have to scrape up $1,000 dollars. Secondly, he didn't really know Avery Deane. In fact, he knew nothing about him except what Deane had told him- that he was a professional ghost writer who had written many books whose titles he wasn't at liberty to divulge. And that he had a kind of undefined relationship to the rug world. Evidently he sometimes bought and sold rugs throughout the world. He spoke familiarly about all the important rug people, though it was hard to tell whether they were friends of his or not.

Anyway, Holden drafted a contract and made Deane read it before he would give him the money. It spelled out their deal in great detail. He had been annoyed when Deane had laughed like a maniac. "A contract? You want me to sign a contract? Ah, good, lad. Very good. That'll do it. Take me to court! Hah, hah!"

"It's just so we have a clear understanding, Avery," he had said. Deane, still laughing, signed without reading it, which gave Holden an unsettled feeling. He gave Deane the money, though. And now, a week later, Deane reappeared, making Holden feel much better. He arose from his roll top desk to welcome him. But a customer walked in right behind Deane and began inspecting rugs on the walls. "Well, Avery will understand if I take care of my customer first," Holden thought, and he gave Deane a high-sign that meant, "Hi, I'll be with you in just a moment but first I have to wait on my customer." It didn't work out that way, though, because Deane got to the customer before Holden did.

"Hah! Good eye!" Deane said, looking over the customer's shoulder at the rug he was studying. "God, you went right to it. Ha, ha, you don't waste time."

"Huh?"

"You went right to the best Bijar in the western states, like a heat-seeking missile. Wham! Oh, I'm sorry; I should introduce: I'm Avery Deane."

"Uh, I'm Tom."

"Hah! Should have known. *Tom.*"

"What do you mean?"

"Thomas Jefferson. Thomas Mann. Thomas Edison. Just to name a few." The customer looked sideways at Avery. "Say," Deane said, "why don't you come with us to Freemont, have a lark?"

Did Holden hear right? Was Deane inviting a customer of his to leave the store? That didn't seem right. Was he going to sell the guy one of his rugs or something? Though feeling shy, Holden interceded. He walked over and said Hi to Deane and the customer.

"All right then, Holden, what's your pleasure? Come with Tom and me to Fremont?"

"Why are you going to Fremont?"

Deane laughed. "R and D, lad. Research and development, and for the best Afghan food outside of Kabul. Qabuli Palau? Afghan Kofta? Lamb kabob? Bouranee Banjan? And nan? Oh, sorry, Tom, this is Holden. Holden, Tom. And that is Holden's famous roll top desk." While Tom glanced at the desk, Deane popped the price tag off the Bijar that Tom had been peering at. Holden saw the move and wondered what was going on. Tom turned back to the rug, probably wondering why his attention had been called to the desk. Avery resumed his hard sell. "So lunch in Little Kabul, right? 'Eat, drink and be merry, for tomorrow we die.' Come on gentlemen, say yes, I'm hungry." Tom shrugged, indecisive. Holden wondered whether he could leave his business. Except for the time he had spent showing Ulysses Pope around, he had maintained his lonely watch over the store from 10 to 5:30, six days a week for three years. Yet what had it gained him? He could put a note in the window. MEDICAL EMERGENCY- back by 3PM. He was getting hungry too. He and Tom said okay at the same time.

"But Tom," Deane said, and took him by the arm and stood close to him, and now his voice dropped to a near whisper, "don't leave that Bijar behind."

"What?" Tom looked uncomfortable. He looked back at the rug on the wall.

Still *sotto voce,* "Buy it, Tom. It's a Bijar, man." His voice rising now, "A Bijar, Tom. Not a sniveling little Chevy, man, but a Bently! A Rolls! It.is.a.one.hundred.year.old.*Bijar,* Tom, and it's a beauty!"

Deane still grasped one of Tom's arms, but Tom appeared not to notice as he stared at the Bijar. With his free hand he gripped a corner of the rug to test its body, then hung on as if he really didn't want to let go. Holden moved in closer to get a better look at the rug he had owned and loved for four years, and now both he and Avery crowded Tom, who had begun to sweat. "Tom," Avery said reasonably, "do the right thing."

"Uh, how much is it?"

"Fif..." Holden began.

"Twenty-five hundred," Avery said. Still Tom clutched the rug in a bulldog grip.

"I'll give you two," Tom said, addressing the offer to Deane.

He laughed, more amused than wounded. "Is that rug a used Nissan, Tom, to be haggled over by desperate people? Tom," Deane explained, "it is a 1924 Rolls Royce Silver Cloud, polished to perfection. Do something good for yourself, Tom, for tomorrow we die." Deane appeared to have become rather emotional at the end. His voice cracked.

Suddenly Tom seemed to be struggling to break out of Deane's grasp and flee, and Holden stood back to give him room, but Tom was only reaching for his wallet. Fifteen minutes later they were all on their way to Little Kabul, riding in Holden's used Nissan.

Of course Little Kabul wasn't Kabul. There was no street in it called Chicken Street, no river winding through it in which women washed clothes, and no wildly painted buses hurtling over rugs left in the street to become antiques in three weeks. But still, you could understand why thousands of immigrants from Kabul had taken up their lives there. As in Kabul, no building rose to more than two or three stories and most hardly rose at all. The town and the land it was on seemed flatter than flat, and yet mountains in the middle distance to the East, and the Pacific Ocean in the West, though not visible, made it seem as if there was a reason for it to have grown up just there. When the three visitors arrived—Tom, the collector, Holden the dealer and Avery Deane the ... what ... dealer? ... collector? ... rug adventurer? ... when they arrived in the center of Little Kabul at lunchtime, they found it blanketed in the same heavy smell of sheep-fat that lay like a coastal fog over Kabul itself.

Avery directed Holden to drive "slowly, slowly" as he looked for a restaurant he seemed to know about. "Here we are!" he shouted. "Park! Park!"

The Marco Polo seemed no more than a café, but certainly it looked authentic. A friendly Afghan waiter suggested this and that. Everything Avery had promised was on the menu. At the end of the meal, the waiter suggested a dish for desert that, when he was asked to explain what it was, he described as "clotted cream." The "clots" were so nearly solid that you could pick them up and eat them with your hand, and that's what Deane did, using only his right hand. Holden thought he had never tasted anything so good.

At the end of it all, Deane went looking for the cook, who also turned out to be the owner. Avery dragged him to their table. "My God man, take the Marco Polo to New York! Take the whole thing to London just like it is! Keep the waiters, keep the menu, keep the furniture, keep your name. You'll be famous. Famous! They'll flock!"

"How about Hollywood?" the cook asked. "You didn't mention Hollywood." Holden and the others looked closer at him. It turned out that he had once lived in Hollywood. His name was Khalil Zadeh and he told them his story.

"This was before the US war against the Taliban. It was before the Taliban. It was before the Russians. It was when Afghanistan was still a happy place and my family of merchants wanted to send a son out to explore the rest of the world. What were the opportunities in America for business, for education, for a good life? So I was selected to investigate since I was unmarried and I spoke some English.

"I landed in the Los Angeles Airport and didn't know where to go next. There was a desk called Visitor Information, and I found a map there of Los Angeles and I sat down and studied it. The only places I had heard of were Hollywood and Venice. I thought my father had probably heard of Hollywood, too, and that he wouldn't like me to go there, and it seemed to me that Venice had something to do with art, so I asked a taxi driver to take me there. Venice Beach. I got out and walked around and couldn't believe what I saw. There was an ocean at the edge of the town and sand around the ocean, and on the sand there were people in swim suits. I had never seen people in bathing suits before. And they were giants, and I mean that. They were huge! I didn't know about weightlifting at that time. They had on little tiny bathing suits, including the women.

"Looking at these people, I was afraid I didn't have what it takes to be an American, but I was determined to try. So as soon as I found a room in Venice Beach, California, I found a place that sold small bathing suits, and I tried to fit in like my father had told me to do. I was never big enough to look like the others down at the beach, though. Still, in clothes I looked a little like the others, with my new gold chains around my neck. I met people and had new friends and learned about snorting cocaine and all of that. So I was getting along pretty well, with money from home. For a while I lived in Hollywood and then I came back to Venice Beach.

"Today there must be two hundred Turkmen people living in America, but at that time I believe I may have been the only Turkmen in the country. I didn't even understand that I was lonely.

"Then I quite writing to my family and one day my father showed up and found me. After the first time he saw those people down at the beach, he refused to look at them. He was a very serious man and soon he found out about AA and got me signed up and pretty soon I'm telling all these strangers, "I am a drug addict." And I was. So it took me all told about twenty years to land here in Little Kabul and open the Marco Polo. So I don't want to go to New York and I don't want to go to London or to Hollywood or Venice. I like it here in Little Kabul. It's hot in the summer and cold in the winter. And there's no beach."

After Holden and Tom and Avery heard Khalil's story, Avery said to him, "You're coming with us. Let's go."

"Let's go where?"

"We're going to find someone who can make a rug."

"We are?" Holden said.

"We are."

"I know where you can buy plenty of rugs," Khalil said, "and they're already made, too."

"No, we want a different kind of rug, one that hasn't been made before."

"I can do that, too. But you have to show me what to make."

"You can? If I show you a drawing of it, can you make it into a graph?"

"Of course I can. Rug making was my family business. We had 600 looms near Andkoi before the Taliban came. I can do it all."

"You can weave?"

"Yes."

"Do you tie with the Persian knot?"

"I tie with the Turkmen knot."

"Hmm. Show me what the Turkmen knot looks like." Khalil showed him by drawing what the knot looked like. Finally Avery said, "That's it! That's what I want, the Persian knot." Khalil shrugged. "You can make graphs and you can weave. Can you dye?"

"Of course I can dye."

"Can you work with natural dyes?" Khalil looked puzzled, so Avery said, "Can you make dyes from roots?"

"No. My mother could, but she's not alive now. I can make dyes from cans."

"Can you spin wool?" Again, Khalil looked blank. "Do you remember how the old ladies used to make yarn?"

Khalil smiled. "Yes, I remember. But no one does that any more. You don't have to. Now you just buy yarn and it's already dyed. It's easier."

"So, Khalil my friend, if I give you a drawing of a rug and the wool already dyed, can you weave a rug for me?"

"How big?"

"Oh, one-and-a-half meters by two meters."

"Yes, I can do that. But first I have to make a loom."

"Can you make a loom?"

"Of course."

"What kind of rug are you going to have Khalil make?" Holden asked.

Avery laughed. "It's a bit embarrassing, lad, but I want a rug with my name in it. Just 'Avery Deane,' that's all."

"Wow," Holden said politely, as if he had never heard of such a good idea.

"Cool," Tom said.

When it was time for Holden and the others to leave, Khalil *baksheeshed* each of them with small Belouch bags— wonderful little pieces that may have been five or ten years old. Deane whispered in Holden's ear, "Lad, be sure to give him a handsome tip."

A tip? Holden hadn't said anything about paying. But he guessed he should. After all, Tom had just bought a rug from him, and Avery had sold it...and he had got $1,000 more for it than he had hoped for. So Holden picked up the bill and left a $25 tip.

"Uh, Avery," he asked, "did the silk Kirman come yet?"

"Hah, hah, hah! Chomping at the bit, are you? Patience, lad. It'll come soon."

Back at the store, Tom picked up his Bijar and left, pleased and excited. Avery paced through the store while Holden excused himself. Holden went through the curtained door to his apartment and to the black hole of Calcutta, and he threw the nice little Belouch bag into it, then a small fistful of moth crystals. When he returned to the showroom, Deane was already in the process of selling his second rug of the day in Holden's store.

"My God man, it's a Jaguar," he was shouting. "A Mercedes. A Porsche 928!"

Chapter Fourteen

Pope was still annoyed, so he let Holden pay for lunch.

 Following a three-day performance at the Halliburton Museum of Fine Arts in Huston, Ulysses Pope flew north-west to repeat his performance at the Denver Fine Arts Museum. It was an act he had perfected during the past decade, and likely there had never been a person as skilled in the art of mau mauing museums as he had become.

He was met at the airport by a senior member of the board of directors of the Denver Fine Arts Museum, a gentleman who had been a low-level general during the Regan administration. The General's aide held a sign at the arrival gate reading **ULYSSES POPE,** and, as soon as Pope revealed himself, the General shook his hand and took his arm and led him to the limousine.

"Sir, we've been looking forward to your arrival. It's not often that a true patron of the arts graces us with a visit. We will do everything we can to make your stay a pleasant one. Of course, as you know, tonight you will be staying in the mayor's mansion and there will be a reception in your honor. I hope we won't tire you with too much attention."

Pope's face was as stony as a gargoyle's, but he felt satisfied with his reception. In the early days, when he was still keeping written scores, he would have given the

General's greeting 90 points. Pope's instinct, though, was to shake things up right from the first. "I don't give a God damned about mayors and mansions and receptions," he said. "Waste of time. What I care about is finding the right home for my collection."

The General was unruffled. "Sir, if you don't mind my saying so, that is the exact phrase we at the Museum use when we're discussing your collection of Oriental rugs. We ask ourselves, how can we create the perfect home for it? And sir, I think we have some answers for you. But I'll let others make the case. I just want to thank you personally for giving us the chance."

Pope would have scored the General's speech rather highly, but he had heard variations of it many times before and pretty much ignored it. He was enjoying the ride in the black stretch-limousine, and, even through the darkened windows he could see motorists and pedestrians gawking at it, no doubt wondering what important person was riding inside. He was looking forward to lavish dinners, a reception in his honor, an attentive mayor, free lodgings in the mayor's mansion, royal treatment by the museum staff and all the other perks accorded to one who had let it out that he was looking for the "right home" for the greatest collection of Oriental rugs in America. He would have plenty of opportunity during the next three days to make nonnegotiable demands (such as to name the Carpet wing of the Museum the Ulysses Pope Heritage), to make important people beg, and to be "shown around" by nubile young docents. And a few days later, he knew, he would take his leave from the museum and its director and its board of directors with a few encouraging words. He would tell them that they were on the right track and that he was impressed by their attitude and that he would discuss all of this with "the boss, hah, hah, hah, Mrs. Pope and see what we come up with." However, he would also mention that the Fogg Museum in Boston had been very receptive, yes, very receptive to some ideas of his, "but we shall see. We shall see." And then he would be on his way to the Los Angeles County Museum of Fine Arts, and finally to the San Francisco Museum to repeat his performance.

Far from exhausting the 84 year old industrialist, the attention paid him by fawning functionaries during his twice-yearly museum tours vitalized Pope, so that by the time he reached San Francisco in the first week of May, he was at the top of his game. As soon he settled into his suite in San Francisco's Ritz Carlton Hotel, provided free, of course, by the San Francisco Museum, he made arrangements concerning his other projects, that is, finding rugs for his collection and recruiting members for his rug group, the International Ali Babba Society. He telephoned the affable young rug dealer in Berkeley named Holden something who, he knew, was running around, possibly right at that moment, arranging a meeting the next night for prospective Ali Babba Society members whom Ulysses Pope would personally address on the subject of Oriental rugs and rug collecting.

The young fellow picked him up the next day at noon as Pope had arranged. Pope suggested a restaurant in San Francisco and Holden drove him there in his modest automobile. Just inside the door of the restaurant, their way was barred by the host, who told Holden that he would not be allowed into the dining room without a necktie. Pope wore his customary suit and tie, and he stood by as an embarrassed and suddenly sweating Holden offered to wait in the car for Pope while he ate lunch, and then accepted a loaner necktie from the host. A moment later the young man came out of the men's room wearing a grotesque necktie in lurid green and yellow. Clearly the tie was meant to punish guests who had showed up without their own neckties.

Seated now and having ordered, Pope went down a mental checklist. "You have a slide projector?

"Yes.

"A screen?"

"Yes."

"A lectern?"

"A lectern?"

"You didn't get a lectern for me?" Pope's young squire looked sick. Pope chuckled to himself and noted how easy it was to make Holden sweat. He hoped the fellow would change his shirt before tonight's meeting, though. Hmm. Maybe he wouldn't have a chance. Pope decided to give him some slack and not make him sweat any more.

"Maybe I didn't mention a lectern. But you do have an audience coming, don't you?'

"About 40 people."

"That's good enough. Well, there's plenty of time until the meeting. There's time for you to take me around." Of course he meant for Holden to take him around from dealer to dealer, just as he had done once before, so Pope could buy rugs from them. This young fellow, Holden, had a store full of good rugs at very good prices, but Pope believed that if he bought more than one or two of them per visit, the kid would realize what he had and would raise his prices. Better to use him as a go-around and pick off his rugs one-by-one, slowly, without driving up his prices. Keep him running around. "If he is back there at his shop he's liable to sell something I want," Pope thought.

As if he were thinking something similar, Holden said, "Uh, I'd better be back at my store by three o'clock. I'm afraid I've left it closed too often lately. But I can take you around to a couple of places here in San Francisco before I have to go."

Pope narrowed his eyes at Holden. "Take my advice, son, and get your priorities straight. You'll make more money that way."

"Uh, I suppose so."

Pope was still annoyed, though, so he let Holden pay the bill for lunch. As the two were leaving the restaurant, the restaurant's host startled Holden by calling after him, "You *are* going to return the tie, aren't you?"

Chapter Fifteen

She threw her arms wide and began singing.
"Somewhere over the rainbow, bluebirds fly..."
She made flying motions with both hands.

 Some of the excited guests sat in a half-circle on rented folding chairs while others stood in small groups, buzzing about Oriental rugs and tonight's speaker. A slide projector faced the screen, and a laser pointer stood by in case the honored rug collector wanted to point out a detail of a rug for the instruction of his audience. And, yes, there was a lectern for him as well, quite a nice oak lectern that was certain to enhance his importance. Somehow Holden had found time and the money to rent it for Ulysses Pope's address.

The audience was somewhat larger than the forty Holden had planned to invite. At the last moment he had invited Avery Deane. Though he was a loose canon, how could Holden not invite him? Avery had now sold nine rugs in Holden's store in a period of about ten days—more than Holden had sold in his own store during the past half-year. Usually Deane sold them for more than Holden's asking price, and always Deane handed over the money to Holden with a flourish. Thinking about him, Holden remembered to invite Tom, the collector who had bought the Bijar and had explored Little Kabul with him and Deane. And then there was the journalist, or perhaps she had said TV journalist, who phoned asking if she could attend Pope's talk. Laura Scott was working on a story, she said, about Pope's famous rug collection. "Yes, of course," Holden said, "come on along. There's plenty of room." So that was forty-three..

The big surprise, though, was a call he had taken late that afternoon from Sarah Atwood, curator of the textile department of the San Francisco Museum. She had heard that Ulysses Pope was speaking that evening and she would like to attend.

"My God," Holden thought, "what is happening to me? Ulysses Pope, Avery Deane and now Sarah Atwood after all my years of obscurity?"

"Well of course you can come, Ms. Atwood. I'd be honored. Actually, we met once before, at a party you put on in Washington, about three years ago, in connection with a show at the Carpet Museum?" She didn't say anything. "It was in your house? I was in a circle that included Mr. Pope and Marley Phillips and Charles Evans Green and you came by and introduced yourself?" She still didn't say anything. "Anyway," he went on, "I was there. So please do come tonight."

"So kind of you," she said. She was guest number forty-four.

And then, finally, also at the last moment, he had phoned Khalil Zadeh, the rug-weaver and chef from Fremont. Holden thought that Khalil might like to be included in a meeting like this. He was almost certain to be the only person there who was an actual rug weaver. Holden had been right. Khalil would love to come, he said, and could bring his wife? "Well, sure," Holden said. Guests number forty-five and forty-six.

Pope and Sarah Atwood had paired off somewhere in the house, probably in the library. Holden knew there was a rumor—Deane had told him, actually—that the San Francisco Museum was trying to land the Pope collection. Maybe that's what they were talking about off by themselves. Still, he felt uneasy. He wondered whether the same man who had pinched the waitress in the Berkeley Marina might try something with Sarah Atwood.

Holden could hear Deane's voice soaring above the scraping of chair legs and the buzz of conversation and laughter. Deane blew over to a guest, intoned a few words and then spun away like a whirlwind to the next. He was heading toward Holden when he literally bumped into Khalil. He seemed surprised to see Khalil. He dropped his voice and said, "Mum's the word, yes?"

"Mum's the word?" Khalil asked. "I don't understand."

Avery put his finger to his lips. "No talking about our little project now. Our little secret, right."

"Okay boss." He winked. Holden joined them, wondering whether Khalil was weaving a rug for Deane. Was that their "little project?" Tom joined the little group. "Hi Holden," Tom said. He nodded at the others. "You should never have sold that Bijar, Holden. I don't think you know how good that rug is. It's a true work of art."

Honestly, Holden hadn't sold very many rugs in his several years in business, but he had sold enough to know by now that, when a collector did buy a rug from him, the collector almost invariably would find some way to crow about it later, as if Holden had made a terrible blunder by selling it at all. So Holden wasn't surprised to hear Tom gloat. What surprised him was Deane's reaction.

"A work of art, Tom? I told you it was a Bentley, a Rolls. I told you it was a beauty. It's those and more, Tom. But it's not a work of art." Deane sounded grumpy, as if Tom had been stupid, and Holden stepped up to defend him, and his Bijar.

"It seems like a work of art to me," he said. "It's a wonderful rug!"

"Oh, *please*, Holden. Is every pretty face a work of art? Is *cute* art? If it's wonderful, pretty, gorgeous, or beautiful does that make it a work of art? You embarrass me, lad."

"Okay, then," Tom spluttered, "what *is* art? If that Bijar isn't art, what *is*?"

"It isn't art, Tom. I just told you."

"He asked a good question, though," Holden said. "So, what is art?"

"Think about a novel," Deane began. He sounded patient, even avuncular, Holden thought, though he detected a certain strain in Deane's voice that reminded him of the very first flutters of a migraine headache. "A good novel creates an illusion. It leads you to believe in a story that never happened. Or think about a stage play or a film. For two hours you're overjoyed or horrified or amused or scared witless. You believe that real life is taking place when all that's actually happening is that actors are speaking lines. And a painting? If it's good enough, you believe that you are looking at George Washington or a field of sunflowers, when, in reality, you are viewing nothing but pigmented oils on a one dimensional surface. A painting is a lie, a fib, a fabrication on canvas." Deane's voice had gradually risen in pitch and volume. People nearby were glancing at him and the others in his group. He looked angry. "A work of art fools you, it takes you out of your everyday reality. That's what all art *does*. Art is artifice. Art is a lie! And that's not what a rug is at all. A rug is a *rug*! Nothing more. It is exactly what it seems to be!" His face was scrunched up like an old crab apple, and he was panting.

"I agree," Khalil chimed in. Holden was astonished. He had barely taken in what Deane was saying and he was a former candidate for an advanced degree in art history. And here was Khalil, an Afghan cook from Fremont, entering the discussion with confidence.

"Hey, art is just stuff that con men make for rich people to hang on their walls. I know an Afghan guy who went to art school here and majored in Corporate Art. That's a good one, isn't it? Corporate art? Is corporate art really art? Yes! That's what art is! It's bunk. It's made to hang on corporate walls; it's cranked out for rich people. That's all it is. *Craft* is better. It's what it seems to be: a beautiful rug for your floor; a great looking mug for your coffee; a wonderful carnelian ring for your finger. Give me craft any day."

"Hah! Spoken like a true craftsman! Our friend Khalil, a weaver of rugs, understands far more about art and craft than our city-boy, educated rug collectors." Avery Deane sneered at Holden, though Holden hadn't said a word.

He was trying to sort it all out when a nice-looking blond woman and a little girl joined their group. Khalil introduced his wife and daughter to the others. Kammy, his wife, clearly was an American. She and Khalil had brought along their daughter, Star—guest forty-seven, Holden calculated. That surprised him, her name and the fact that they had brought her, but, "Why not?" he thought. "Star might enjoy Pope's talk, too." The little girl was cute. She was so cute that it caused Holden some consternation. "Seven going on 23," he thought. Huge brown Afghan eyes, full dark brown hair in long, disturbing, Shirley Temple ringlets. Deane and Holden and Tom all said hello to the mother and daughter.

Ulysses Pope was still huddled with Sarah Atwood somewhere in the big house. Holden's guests, who had gathered to hear the great Pope speak about rugs, were beginning to tire. Most had found seats by now and had gradually found less and less to talk about with their neighbors. Now they were beginning to look over their shoulders to see if Pope was on his way. It was nine o'clock and soon baby sitters would expect them home with $20 and a ride.

Khalil called out to Holden from where he and his family were seated, "Shall Star sing, Holden? She can sing for everyone while we wait." Holden saw that Kammy, Star's mother, was perfectly ready to give up her daughter for the entertainment of the guests. Several of the members of the audience said "Yes!" and the matter was decided on.

Holden said, "Sure. Come on up, Star, what will you sing?" Suddenly Star was up in front of everyone, wearing a professional smile and a layer of confidence. She did not wear makeup but her dark, sultry eyes suggested mascara. She threw her arms wide and began singing. "Somewhere over the rainbow, bluebirds fly..." She made flying motions with both hands. The seven-year-old belted out her number like a Las Vegas pro. Everyone must have been as confused as Holden by her performance. Surely this girl had one of those moms who coach and prod and venture their daughters into fame. Or was it an encouraging father, Holden wondered, a father who had landed in Venice Beach, California direct from Afghanistan and who had also done some time in Hollywood? By the end of Star's performance, all the men were smiling strained smiles and looking away from the girl. The women in the audience were nodding toward her in approval, but Holden wondered what they really thought. All clapped and yelled things like "Yes!" and "Hooray!"

That's when Ulysses made his entry. Maybe he had been waiting all this time for applause, but, anyway, he took advantage of it and walked up an aisle to the lectern, dignified, like a keynote speaker at a graduation ceremony. The guests were satisfied that they had not waited in vain.

Reading from notes, Pope began by talking about his own interest in rugs, how he had become interested in them as a young engineer in the oilfields around Abbadan in southern Iran. He told amusing stories about how he had learned to bargain like "an Arab," and how he had often bested Middle Eastern rug traders at their own game. In a rug-buying trip through Turkey he had conspicuously carried prayer beads that would have identified him to the natives as a fellow Muslim, and which, he was convinced, earned him better treatment and far lower prices in the bazaars. And then he described his "last-day-in-town" strategy. He had noticed that no matter how hard he bargained during his stay in a town, during the last few hours of his stay, right before the taxi showed up at his hotel to take him to the airport, the price of rugs fell by another 30%. So eventually he trained himself to take on that last day in town attitude on the *first* day he was in any rug center.

Admittedly—that is to say, even Holden would have admitted it—this part of Pope's address went on way too long. It is true that some of his audience took notes as he talked: "Prayer beads," they wrote; "Last-day-in-town." But others seemed puzzled. Wasn't he going to talk about Oriental rugs? But he got to that. He told how he had found a Saryk engsi ("Pende katchli" he called it) at the bottom of a cobwebby stack of rugs in the London Free Port and had paid 165 pounds for it and it was worth $8500. He enumerated many other such triumphs. Of course Holden was happy for him and so must others have been. But he knew that the rug collectors and dealers sitting in their folding chairs around the great man were used to a pretty high caliber of rug scholarship in their San Francisco and Berkeley rug circles and that they would be expecting something better from Ulysses Pope. And they would expect it pretty soon because it was 10 o'clock and they were tired.

But he moved right to his pitch. "The Ali Babbas," he said, "are everywhere. I've founded branches in every major European rug center and, of course, in New York, Chicago, Boston, Charleston, and Los Angeles. Finally I have time to establish a branch in San Francisco and I am asking you to become charter members of our fraternity. You will be able to visit meetings of the Ali Babbas anywhere you travel. You will be connected with the rug world wherever you are, and you will receive copies of *The Ali Babba*, our newsletter which I personally write. Dues are a nominal $200 per year. I ask you to pick up applications at the end of my talk, fill them out if you would like to join, and give them to me along

with a check for $200 before you leave. And now goodnight."
To applause, Pope ceased talking and stood aside from the
lectern, waiting to be approached by those wanting his
attention. He had takers, people who always wanted to
engage the famous. Others, who were sensitive to people's
needs, believed that the old man was failing and crying out
for support of some kind and they waited in a little line to
shake his hand and assure him that he had really stirred
them and that they would like to join his club.

Holden was surprised that was all there was to it.
"Hmmm," he thought. "Well, he's quite old. On the other
hand, he wasn't too old to pinch a waitress." But, before he
could sort it all out, Holden had to shake hands with the
many weary-looking people he had invited to tonight's
festivities as they thanked him for a "wonderful night."
Khalil, Kammy and Star left first. Star had fallen asleep and
Khalil carried her out. Deane looked sour and didn't say
much. Others, like Tom, were very polite. The media
person—journalist?—was not so polite. Laura Scott.

"Well, he's a bore," she said, tilting her head toward Pope,
but she didn't seem to hold Holden responsible. She looked
weary too, but she was friendly to Holden. "I thought he
would be a jerk and I wasn't disappointed. Are you all right?"

Holden laughed. Was he all right? Why wouldn't he be?
Still, he felt relieved by her question. "I'm all right," he said,
"but it sure has been a long day." She laughed, too, as if he
and she understood something together.

Eventually they all left except Pope. Sarah Atwood had
been the last. She had lingered, talking earnestly with the old
rug collector till the last moment, and then finally it was just
a tired-to-the-bones Holden and a Ulysses Pope who seemed

neither more nor less lively than ever. Holden broke down the projector screen and removed the slides from the rented projector and folded the metal chairs and cleaned up while Pope put filled-in membership applications and checks in his briefcase. While he was still working, Holden said politely, "Well, I'm sure convinced, Mr. Pope. I'd like to join the Ali Babbas. I already filled out my application. Should I write a check right now or what?" Pope continued to sort his notes and he placed them carefully in his briefcase, but he said nothing. "Mr. Pope?" He still didn't answer. Holden felt so tired. This had been a strange time for him. He had been visited by the angels, the rug angels. They had descended on him, evidently meaning him well. They had brought him *sales*, the life's blood and validation of anyone who had chosen to make his living with Oriental rugs. They had brought him *status* among his colleagues and customers, the essential component of respect and even self-respect. The presence of the angles seemed to suggest that suddenly he had *connections*, in the Museum, for instance, and maybe even in the *media*! Perhaps he had turned the corner. He had emerged! But, on the other hand, since the angels had descended upon him, he had been putting signs on his shop's door saying things like, "Closed due to illness," or, sometimes, just "Open Tomorrow, 9 to 5:30." Closing during business hours went against every instinct that keeping a shop had instilled in him. And racing around trying to keep these prima donnas like Deane and Pope happy was a strain. So it was a time for Holden that promised much but that left him on infirm ground. Besides which he had paid for every goddamned lunch and dinner and rental lectern and whatever for the past three weeks!

117

Was he grouchy from all of this? "Mr. Pope? Did you hear me? I'd like to join the Ali Babbas." Finally Pope looked up at him.

"The Ali Babbas don't admit rug dealers," he said. He put another thing or two in his leather briefcase and then again looked up at Holden. "I thought you knew that."

Chapter Sixteen

Holden's swearing was clumsy but heart-felt.

As a boy Holden had fought to stay awake. Eyes leaden and his mouth drooly from exhaustion, he had steeled himself against sleep. Why? Because he wanted to stay awake and have some more fun. He had loved having fun so much as a boy that he had kept on playing even when he was sick. He would burn with fever, would even know he was quickly becoming ill, but he kept on playing rather than go home and go to sleep. His parents misunderstood and believed that he was an irresponsible child or even a bad boy. But he just wanted to have a little more fun before he had to give up playing.

But after the party he organized for Ulysses Pope, he wanted nothing so much as to sleep. He wanted to sink his head into his pillow and stop thinking and drift into sleep. But he couldn't.

Ulysses Pope had so naturally and so easily put him in his place that Holden almost agreed he belonged there. Evidently Holden had missed a fact of life that was clear to Pope and maybe to everyone but him: There are gentlemen and there are shopkeepers. Shopkeepers are not gentlemen and they are not invited to join the social circles of those who are. He had missed it. Or maybe he had known it dimly from echoes in the air of ancestral attitudes. "Anyway," he told himself, "I should have known."

Lying in his bed, Holden laughed bitterly. For a few heady days, he had believed that he was being welcomed into the circle of the rug-world's high and mighty. Believing that he had been "discovered," he had begun to believe that success was knocking on the door. Could it be that all he needed now to be successful was to adjust his prices or beat the bushes for even better rugs or stay open longer hours or send newsletters to his customers or have Christmas specials? But when Ulysses Pope looked up at him and said, "I thought you knew," Holden suddenly understood that he had been mistaken. Yes, he might manage to make a go of his business, but it did not follow that he was in the circle, the "fraternity," Pope had called it, or that he ever could be.

And Sarah Atwood. Had he really presumed to fantasize about her? (He had.) No wonder she had ignored him at her party in Washington and then tonight at his own party for Pope. It was a matter of class. Holden's face burned as he thought about it. No wonder they had all ignored him except insofar as it was handy to have him "take them around" or to have him pay for their meals.

Holden flung back the covers and left his bed. He went to the black hole of Calcutta and sat looking into it. He sat in the dark, and the old laundry shoot was dark too, so there was nothing to see. But he peered into it anyway, thinking, "Somewhere down there are the bags and bands and tassels and rugs and the odds and ends of my career. The freebies, the gifts, the things I've saved for a rainy day. The bag Khalil gave me is down there. And before that? What was it I tossed down just before that?" Suddenly sleepy, Holden couldn't remember.

"Idiot," he mumbled. "Dip stick," he said. He was thinking of Ulysses Pope, half-dreaming. "Puffed up old lecher. Pincher. Cheapskate." Even in his slumber, Holden was gaining conviction. "Take your*self* around, you old fart. Screw you. Eat shit." Holden's swearing was clumsy but heart-felt. He took a breath, then went back to bed. And just before he slept he thought, "Didn't something tell me from the first that they weren't wonderful people? Just because I admired them doesn't mean I should have."

Holden awoke the next morning wondering about Avery Deane. Avery too had let Holden pay for every meal. Holden had had to drive *him* around, too—to Little Kabul, for instance. "For all his talk about how my prices are too low,'" Holden observed, "I notice that he hasn't bought a single rug from me. Why not?" Holden mused for a moment. "I didn't see in time what Pope is, but even a dope like me can learn," he thought. "I know him now, but what about Deane? Who is he? What is he? A con man? What am I going to learn about Deane that I should already have guessed? Where is the silk Kirman that should have come two weeks ago?"

By three that afternoon, thirty-eight of the people who had been at Holden's party the night before, including Deane, had either given Ulysses Pope their application for membership in the Ali Babba Society or had phoned Holden saying that their application was in the mail. They were all going to join. They seemed excited. Holden thanked them.

The last call of the day was from Laura Scott. "I'd like to interview you for a story I'm writing about Oriental rugs. Would you have an hour or so for me to ask you a few questions?"

"Well, sure," he said.

"Right after work this evening?"

When Laura showed up at the store at 5:30, she brought a bottle of Chateau-Neuf-de-Pape and a baguette. "I thought this might hit the spot after a day at work," she said. "And who knows, wine has been known to loosen the tongue. Maybe you can give me some good tips for my story." Holden smiled and felt tired. She was looking at rugs on the showroom walls as Holden stepped through the curtain and then to his kitchen and found two wine glasses, a cork-screw and a bread knife. He returned to his guest in the showroom.

"What a lovely atmosphere for an interview," she said. They sat side by side on a stack of rugs, and another, higher stack of rugs became their table. "Thank you for letting me come to your party last night. I wanted to see Ulysses Pope in his own world. My story is about collecting rugs, and he is said to be the country's most important collector."

"Yeah," he said, without spirit.

She looked at him. "I keep hearing rumors that he's going to give his collection to the San Francisco Museum."

He looked glum. "Uh, listen, I have to make a confession. Just because Pope had me run around and put together an audience for his talk last night doesn't mean that he tells he anything. I sure don't have any inside information."

Laura poured a glass of wine for Holden and sawed off a quarter of the baguette for him. "Well then, let's not talk about the old geezer. I don't like him anyway." Holden laughed. "Is anyone who was there last night going to join Ali Babba and the Forty Thieves?" she asked.

Holden laughed again and took a sip of wine. "They're *all* going to join. People have been coming in all day, dropping off their applications, or they've phoned, saying that their applications are on the way or they gave Pope their applications last night."

"Well," she said, "there's one born every minute." Holden wondered what she knew about Pope. "But," she went on, "maybe you can tell me something about collecting rugs. That's what I'm writing about, what makes a rug collector tick. As a dealer you must have some insight into the minds of rug collectors."

The wine was good. He tore off a piece of his bread and dipped it in his glass and popped the reddened bread in his mouth. Then he wondered whether you're supposed to do that. Probably not, he decided. Still, she hadn't glowered or anything. "Well," he said, "that's another thing I don't know anything about, collectors' minds. In three years I haven't sold more than two- dozen rugs to collectors. I guess my only wisdom about collectors is that they don't want to buy from me." Once more he laughed. "They all like to show me what they bought sight-unseen from some guy in London or what they got on the internet from someone who lied to them."

"Why do you suppose that is?"

"Beats me. Maybe I'm not a very good salesman."

"Well you sure don't toot your own horn."

Holden watched her break off a piece of baguette and dip it in her wine and then down it. He was *washed* in relief and gratitude. "You mean I don't promote myself? But isn't it rude to go around bragging?"

Now it was Laura who laughed. "You're unusual, you know."

"Yeah?"

"Yes. Most people who are interviewed have one thing in mind: to promote themselves. They want a plug. They want to look good. They want to be a star."

"I didn't think of it."

"You just told me that a famous man doesn't confide in you and that collectors don't buy rugs from you. How are you going to become a star that way?"

Holden knew she was kidding him and he knew that at the same time she was telling him something important. He was kind of tickled by the conversation, but the talk about himself was making him uncomfortable. He said, "So are you going to join the Ali Babbas?"

"Of course not. Ulysses Pope is a jerk. I wouldn't have anything to do with him except to observe him where he feeds and to take notes."

"Where he feeds?"

"You talk about self-promotion! That's all he does," she said. "He fattens himself on people. Of course it's their own fault. They hope to profit from him."

Holden was silent, wondering where he fit into *that* picture. Laura seemed to have become serious. Maybe even angry. He said, "I disagree. He does more than just promote himself. Sometimes he pinches people."

She turned to him and took his arm. "Oh my God! He pinched *you*, too?"

"What? No. He pinched a cocktail waitress. For goodness sake, he didn't pinch me!"

"Well you're lucky!"

"Wait! You mean that old son of a bitch..."

"Forget about it."

"Wait! What are you saying?"

After more talk along these lines, Holden and Laura went out for pizza.

Pope had pinched her in an elevator. "I was doing publicity for the Halliburton Museum of Fine Arts and I was assigned to show him around the museum and make sure he was happy and get him coffee or alcohol or whatever he wanted. The museum was trying to land his collection of rugs. So in the elevator on the way to the lunchroom, he made a pass at me. I mean, physically. I couldn't believe it. It was disgusting. It didn't bother him a bit that I was furious. He was proud of himself. So I know all about that old jerk, and it's not over yet."

"What do you mean?"

"I mean that he'll be sorry for ever touching Laura Scott." They had opened a second bottle of wine with dinner. Laura was steamed. "Here's what I've learned about him so far," she said. "He promises his collection to the Halliburton. They treat him like royalty. He promises his collection to the museum in Denver. They treat him like royalty. He promises his collection to the San Francisco Museum and they treat him like royalty. He's got it figured out so that everyone treats him like a king. I'm going to blow the whistle."

"Blow the whistle?"

"Watch for it. The New Yorker. The New York Times. Sooner or later one of them will publish an amusing article exposing him. And my name will be on the byline."

"Exposing him for what?"

"I would think it would be enough to call attention to his museum scam, promising all of them his collection. But maybe you're right. Maybe I have to get more on him. I'm still digging. But tell me, did *you* join Ali Babba and the Forty Thieves?"

That's the question Holden had been dreading. "No," he said.

"Then I'm proud of you! Why didn't you join?"

"Uh…" Holden thought about lying. He was ashamed that he had wanted to join. He was ashamed that he hadn't been allowed to join. She was not going to be proud of him. "Uh, he wouldn't let me. He said that dealers weren't allowed to join. He said he thought I knew that."

Laura turned to him and took his arm. "Are you kidding? He didn't let you join? After you got the talk together for him?"

"Yes."

"Did he ask you to gather people for his talk or was it your idea?"

"He asked me."

"And he wouldn't let you join?" Holden didn't answer. He felt like an idiot.

A half hour later Laura was still furious about how the old man had treated him. Holden had stopped thinking about it though. He was just thinking about the way Laura still had hold of his arm. He was starting to like the way her eyes flashed. He liked the way her mouth looked when she turned to him.

As Holden drove her back to the shop where she had parked her car, Laura said, "Since you claim not to have any insight into the mind of rug collectors, would you give me a list of the collectors who were at the meeting last night so that I can interview them?" He felt something that was reasonably close to jealousy but said yes and gave her the guest list before she left.

"They all quit," she said. Three days later she called him and told him the news.

"What?"

"I phoned all of them and told them what the old man did to you and they all quit. They were horrified. Everyone thinks Pope was very shabby to you. They all assumed that you would be in the club, too. A lot of them said they had joined *because* of you. So they all quit. They stopped payment on their checks. They sent letters to him in protest. They all dropped out."

"They what?"

"Quit."

"All of them?" Holden was trying to take it in. "Avery Deane?"

For a moment, Laura didn't answer. "Well, Deane couldn't wait to quit. I think he despises Pope. But no," she said, "one of them didn't quit. Sarah Atwood was the exception. She seemed to think it was none of my business, and she said she had 'full confidence' in Ulysses Pope. That was after she found out I am a journalist."

Holden was struggling with his feelings. He kind of hated to see Pope embarrassed this way. But he was so surprised by what Laura had done and so grateful to all the people who had dropped out.

"The thing I learned from all of this," she went on, "was how much everyone likes you and respects you. They all had great things to say about you. So I don't know why they won't buy your rugs. They all said you have wonderful rugs. The impression I got was that they all wanted to buy rugs and bring them to you so you would approve of them. That's pretty strange, isn't it?"

Holden didn't know what to think so he just said, "I guess it was pretty dumb of me to dip bread in my wine the other night. Thank you for making it seem all right. I really liked the way you held on to my arm and I liked your eyes and your mouth. Do you suppose we could have a date?"

"Well, sure," she said.

Chapter Seventeen

He was pulling at his hair, evidently in a kind of ecstasy.
His voice had risen to a thrilling shout.

 Avery Deane's landlady, Sandra Smith, hadn't been born yesterday, not at all, and when exotic looking women began climbing the stairs to his studio apartment, she knew there was going to be trouble. Two, three, and finally four dark-eyed women entered Deane's studio apartment, just above her own. Not that she was old fashioned. She had never told her guests that they couldn't have company of the opposite-sex, but four women wearing veils? Not veils like Shaharazade but scarves pulled over their heads to make them look sexy, or maybe to make them hard to identify in a police line-up. They all had big brown eyes and looked like they might be exotic dancers. Some of them carried...instruments. Wooden *things* possibly involving torture; that or they looked a little like spinning wheels.

Inside her own apartment, she peered at her ceiling and listened for dancing or ecstatic shouts from above, but she heard nothing. She climbed the stairs and, in the hallway above, walked slowly past her tenant's door. It was ajar but the light inside was so dim that she could make out nothing, and she walked on. When she was just a few feet further down the hallway, she heard his booming voice behind her.

He sounded excited. "My dear, would you like to see something interesting?" She stopped and looked around as if she couldn't imagine who was talking to her, then glanced over her shoulder and seemed surprised to see Deane.

"Ah, Mr. Deane, my head was in the clouds, you might say. I didn't even know you were home."

"And what a home it is, too. *Feels* like home, the nice way you furnished it with the doilies and all. Wonderful way to live. I owe you, dear. But do come and meet my spiritual teachers."

"Spiritual teachers, Mr. Deane?"

"Salt of the earth. You'll love them. Do come in." Deane's right arm swept the air before the door to his castle and Sandra followed his gallant flourish. Inside, Deane's voice rang, "Mrs. Smith, please meet my gurus, my teachers, my guides: Zainab, Soroya, Katija and Fatima. Ladies, please welcome Mrs. Smith, a gifted interior designer." Four pairs of big brown eyes looked up, though not the eyes of harlots, as she had imagined them, but the soulful eyes of peasants— was that the right word? Country people, anyway, she thought. People from some other country. They were sitting on pillows on the floor and were working or making ready to work at what, after all, could only be spinning wheels. The women smiled soft, doughy smiles at her. No, they were not women of ill repute.

So Mr. Deane liked the way she had decorated his furnished apartment! She had always taken pride in decorating each apartment individually, though not every one of her tenants over the years had seemed to appreciate it. This apartment was what she thought of as the doily unit. Most of her guests were ladies, and she had had them in mind when she gathered every piece of fancy lace she had ever owned—from under her bed and from ancient trunks in her attic and from high closet shelves—to make this room special. She had draped a lacy old tablecloth over the back of the brown mohair sofa, for instance, and she had deployed doilies nearly everywhere, sixty, eighty, maybe a hundred of them! She placed them on the tops of dressers and on the dining room side table, on the coffee table, on the dining room table, on the bed. She even put all the waste-paper baskets on doilies. And Mr. Deane seemed to love them! "Feels like home," he had said. What a pleasant man.

Sandra Smith smiled at the brown-eyed women sitting bare-footed on the floor. They had begun to work. One turned her wheel, faster and faster now, while her partner played out a stream of wool fibers that soon became a long and ever-growing strand of yarn that wound onto the whirling spindle. "The ancient art of spinning, Mrs. Smith! May I call you Sandra? They're teaching me its mysteries," Deane said, beaming, "and through spinning I hope to glean the eternal spiritual truths, just as Mahatma Ghandi did. The Afghans owned the skill before Alexander the Great explored their country, Sandra. They could spin three thousand years before Gengis Khan invaded their homeland. And I? Hah, hah, hah!" He laughed at himself dismissively. "I sometimes feel clever because I can balance a check book or pass a driver's test. But can I work this magic? Make woolen yarn from a sheep's back? Not I. But I can learn! I can learn!" Sandra wondered whether she too could learn how to spin. The ladies hunkering there on the floor seemed so... centered. It all seemed like so much fun, and Mr. Deane's enthusiasm was catching. Avery, she would call him Avery.

"Well what do you think, Sandra? Shall we lend a hand? Spindle's nearly full. Maybe we should bundle the yarn up into skeins. Perhaps they'll show us how."

"Oh yes," she said, and she kicked off her shoes. "Maybe they'll show us how."

The day passed pleasantly, and she learned so much. "Where did the wool come from, Mr. Deane? Avery. Did they really cut it off a sheep's back?"

"Wrong kind of sheep here, my dear. I ordered Chinese wool. The best. The best! Gorgeous, buttery stuff. Our friends here didn't clip it, but rather an industrious Chinese shepherd did. Bloody U.S. Customs Service did their best to sabotage my shipment. Couldn't figure out how to classify it for duty so they were ready to send it back to China. Bloody fools."

Sandra Smith had noticed that Avery could be quite up-and-down. He could snarl. Then, the next thing you know, he's as excited as a kid and he's got everyone running around doing things and having fun.

"What will happen to the wool once they teach you how to spin it?" she asked. "Look how much there is already!"

"Well then, we'll have to learn to dye it, won't we? Roots, fruits, bark and all that good stuff. Grind it all up and let it boil for a few days. Then we plop in all that nice wool and we have something."

"My goodness! You're going to learn to dye the wool as well? From fruits and roots?"

"And bark. Bit of a problem, though. There's no one around who knows how to do it. Of course it's a cinch with synthetic dyes—anyone can do that. But I've only heard of one person in America who is really expert at dyeing with natural substances."

"Why, who is that, Avery?" As she and Deane talked, his spiritual teachers continued to turn out an impressive quantity of hand-spun wool.

"Woman in Oregon. A witch. Casts spells and all that. But she knows how to use natural dyes and can even dye a specific color from Mother Nature's bounty."

"Hmmm. Is she going to be your spiritual guide, too?"

"If I can find her." Suddenly Avery stopped winding wool into skeins and stood straight. He looked at Sandra as if surprised to see her. "Why that's it, my dear. You can help me look for her. We'll have a lark! Oregon! I've never been there!"

"Why Mr. Deane!"

"Cherise Hollander, that's her name. Said to live in the woods somewhere around Coos Bay. I'm sure we can find her. How many witches could there be in Oregon?"

What a time! They drove up the Pacific coast in Sandra's car. (Why had they decided to take hers? She couldn't remember.) What a time they had had in ridiculous but at least cheap little motels—which was good because it always seemed to happen that Avery was somewhere else when it came time to pay. What a time they had had asking here and there in Oregon about a witch named Cherise Hollander. And finally they had crunched up a long gravel driveway lined with conifers, tooting the horn to announce their approach to the lonely cabin. No need to surprise someone who, startled, might cast a spell on intruders. And now it seemed as if they had found her. A woman stood before the door of her cabin and watched them approach. She neither wore a pointed hat nor did she have a pointed chin, and, though a cat sat beside her looking at the strangers, it was a calico. The woman was soft and mild and vague-looking in loose-fitting, hand loomed clothes of tasteful colors, a shawl around her shoulders. Deane eased the car to within a few yards of where she stood and turned off the motor. He rolled down his window and a smell of conifers and high mountains blew into Sandra's car.

"Have we found you then?" Deane called to the witch. "Cherise Hollander?" When she neither answered nor moved, he went on. "It is said, my dear, that you have unlocked the secrets of natural dyes and we have come to learn from you."

She considered. "I'm not taking students," she said.

"Apprentices, then: two learners who will clean up after you for scraps of wisdom." Sandra wasn't so sure she wanted to become an apprentice. After all, she would have to get back home before long. She was hoping that Avery could work out something short of an apprenticeship.

The woman smiled. "Scraps of wisdom?" She shook her head and invited them to come in.

She had soon heated a brimming kettle-full of vegetable soup. Fresh-looking, leafy garden things floated in its bubbling broth. Sandra examined them suspiciously, but Avery Deane ploughed into his soup with relish. "The earth's bounty," he said between spoons full. "Homegrown! Fresh from the garden soil." Then, "Earthworms!" Sandra recoiled in horror from her bowl, confirmed in her worst fears. But Deane went on, "Earthworms. Those natural tillers of the soil! What a job they've done to the soil in which these vegetables grew. Health! Nature's bounty, not so, Sandra? Ah, the good life!" For a moment Sandra felt almost jealous. He seemed nearly as enthusiastic about this witch's soup as he had about her own doilies. But soon Sandra herself began to notice just how fresh and tasty the soup was, and she lost her thoughts about earthworms and her jealousy as she gave herself to nature's bounty.

"Yum," she said aloud.

After lunch, while they sat and chatted, Sandra noticed that Avery eyed Cherise's homespun clothes.

Suddenly he jumped up. "My God, "it *is* true, isn't it? Your clothes! You've made them yourself, haven't you? And their colors—how they glow—you've dyed them from nature, haven't you? By God, I can't stand it!" He was pulling at his hair, evidently in a kind of ecstasy. His voice had risen to a thrilling shout. "And see here!" He had taken a corner of her shawl. "You're *wearing* a textile that should be admired by thousands ! *Wearing* it when it could be in a museum! Lock it up!" he cried. "Lock it up, lass. Mount it, frame it, photograph and publish it, but lock it up!

Sandra noticed Cherise's shawl for the first time. It *was* pretty, like hippy clothes from the 60's, but this one was really good. Even Cherise looked down at it—at her own shawl—and seemed surprised to see what a fine thing it was. She stroked it appreciatively, but soon she peered closer at Deane, who was stomping about like Rumpelstiltskin.

"I can say a few words that will make you feel much better," she told him. "Or I can brew something special for you."

He calmed down right away. It was a good thing, too, because Sandra had resolved that there was no way she could let him take something the witch gave him. But he appeared to have had the same thought, and he carefully backed away from Cherise. "No, no," he said. "But really, dear, I can't tell you how much I admire your work with natural dyes. I mean, if you aren't taking students, well, I wonder whether you might be interested in dyeing some wool for us. Handspun Chinese wool. It's in the car."

"A commission?"

"Yes, yes, a commission. But a difficult one, because the wool will have to be dyed particular colors, you understand? I have six very particular colors in mind."

"What for?"

"Why, for nothing, dear. For the lovely colors. For fun, you might say. For love! For truth! For beauty!" He was beginning to get wound up again.

"Maybe you'd better show me the colors you have in mind."

"Splendid. But all I have to show you is a few photographs."

"Of?"

"Of old rugs, dear. Old Chinese rugs."

"Oh I can do those. That's where I started, 20 years ago. The colors in old Chinese carpets. I can do them in my sleep. Would you like to see my garden?" That's when Sandra found out where all those leafy and twiggy things in the soup came from, and all the roots and fruit skins and whatever that Cherise made her dyes from. Right there beside her cabin. It was a wonderful garden, but not a single thing in it looked familiar to Sandra.

Four days later, when it was time to settle up with Cherise for the sixty skeins of wool she had dyed to order from natural substances, Avery was tromping around in the woods somewhere and Sandra wrote a check. $450. But she decided not to worry about it. She was having the time of her life.

Chapter Eighteen

*He could no more remember learning to weave
than he could remember learning to eat.*

 Khalil Zadeh glanced up at his drawing of Avery Deane's rug and tied another knot, then another and another and another, and after each knot he cut the yarn with a flick of his crescent-shaped knife. It had taken nearly three weeks for his hands to begin working fluidly at the loom as they had when he was a boy in northern Afghanistan. Like nearly all Turkmen children, he had hunkered beside his mother at the loom and had *absorbed* rug making. He could no more remember learning to weave than he could remember learning to eat. Still, he had not sat at a loom in twenty years, so for the first three weeks he had struggled to find his old rhythm.

The design Deane had given him made it even harder to settle into his work. It was not at all like the Turkmen designs he had woven as a youth. And, worse, day after day he had to stare into the eyes of a dragon that emerged knot by knot before him, and each night he dreamed about the dragon's eyes. They seemed to ask, "Who are you, Khalil? Are you still a Turkmen, a son of the Central Asian Steppes? Or are you an American restaurant owner, a father whose daughter has a future in Hollywood? Are you an immigrant?

A refugee? Are you traveling in disguise? Are you still a Turkmen?" Then, finally, he had woven his way past the dragon and he no longer had to look it in the eye.

And the colors: They were not the familiar bright red and blue-black of Turkmen rugs. Avery had given him yarn dyed amber and yarns in light, medium and deep blue, and others in gold and russet. And worse: the yarn itself was lumpy and uneven, thick here and skinny there and unfamiliar in his hands. He knew it was the work of Afghan women he had recommended, friends from little Kabul who still remembered the old way of spinning wool on spindles, but secretly he believed the hand spun wool to be inferior to the machine spun wool he had worked with as a boy.

And yet, for all that, Khalil had begun to enjoy himself, for his rhythm was coming back to him, and gradually he began to remember how he had felt as a child in Afghanistan and Pakistan when he had had no doubts about who he was.

People came to watch him weave. Avery Deane was often by his side and he seemed peaceful during these times. Deane's landlady, Sandra, sometimes sat with him and together they watched Khalil at his loom. Sometimes his Afghan friends, Kadija, Zinab, Soroya, and Fatima, long since finished with their spinning, came to watch the rug grow. So from time to time there would be seven people and a loom in Deane's studio apartment, yet it was a quiet and peaceful time for Khalil and his friends. Everyone seemed deep in thought.

As Khalil wove, he remembered the time when his father had decided to break down the family yurts in northern Afghanistan and move to Pakistan's North-West Frontier. His family had been among the first Afghans to flee their homeland when, already by 1978, the Russians became a gray presence in Afghanistan. They were a presence to which Khalil's people, the Turkmen, were especially sensitive, for just a hundred years earlier the Turkmen had been the last of the tribes of the Central Asian steppes to be "settled" by the Russians. Being settled had meant an end to their ancient, semi-nomadic life. Now, a hundred years later, the Russians had drawn even further south and were in a settling mood again, and Khalil's father decided to leave.

After the tents were packed, there was no room for the sixty looms that had been the tools of the family's rug trade. Instead, the family itself—Mother, Khalil and five brothers and sisters and Uncle Hajji—packed themselves into the remaining cargo space of their 1956 Russian-made truck. So, as the autumn of 1978 was deepening, Father steered south through the Salang Pass and then south-east toward the Pakistani border, Mother and children bundled in the back, festive at first and then tired and irritated. They traveled on roads that weren't exactly roads and they tried to avoid checkpoints manned by Russian soldiers in gray uniforms.

They traveled barely faster than the camel caravans they slowly overtook, and often, when the truck broke down and Father and Uncle Hajji leaned over the engine and rigged repairs from smoke and mirrors, the camel trains they had passed hours before caught up and overtook them.

Khalil, who was twelve years old, was tormented by an absolutely unrelenting erection, brought on by the constant jiggling and bumping and grinding of the low-geared old truck and by hormones of which he had no understanding and over which he had no control. Luckily he was clad in loose-fitting clothes and his secret, he hoped, was safe, but he could hardly endure his condition.

They bypassed Kabul to avoid Russians and after eight days of travel began to ascend the Khyber Pass. Khalil peered at what seemed to be earthen fortresses high above the road and imagined that men with rifles looked down upon their slow progress. And finally they were on the desert plains outside of Peshawar and they were passing occasional tents along the road and people they spoke with told them that they had arrived. Mother disagreed. She would have nothing to do with the camp life where people unknown to each other just minutes before—people of questionable ethnicity and religion—established their homes within a few feet of each other. Khalil knew her to be decisive in her opinions, and now he learned that she was also powerful, for she insisted that Father keep driving and he did. They reached the no-man's-land between Afghanistan and Pakistan, and then they passed through it, too, and lumbered into Peshawar. There she had Father rent a room in a house in the city and finally they all climbed out of the truck's bed and straggled into the room and found spots on the floor to unroll Turkmen rugs on which they collapsed, exhausted.

For the next three years the nine refugees spent their nighttime hours together in that room, cooking, praying and teaching or learning rudimentary reading and math. During daylight hours, those who could—that is, everyone over 10 years old, including Khalil—wove rugs in small manufactories in Peshawar. The younger children played near Mother as she hunkered at a horizontal loom and tied knots. In that way, by the end of a year, the family had bought six looms and had contracted weavers to make rugs which Father could sell for a small profit. After another year of hard work and thrift, they owned eighteen looms, and by the time they moved from Peshawar at the end of three years, they had 38 looms and sixty fellow Turkmen refugees dyeing, weaving and finishing rugs for the family business.

Most Pakistanis in Peshawar treated them like dogs. They regarded the growing tribes of refugees as a big problem. Pakistani policemen seized their papers and made them pay to get them back. For a brief time, Uncle Hajji was held in jail, accused of being a "spy." Khalil's family decided to move to Lahore. Uncle Hajji stayed in Peshawar to supervise the looms.

In Lahore, things improved for Khalil. He was able to go to school and he learned English and other things that interested him. At the same time, now fifteen, he became more and more important in his family's carpet business. His father sent him over the border into Afghanistan to buy superior Ghazni wool and to smuggle it back into Pakistan. It was often his job to bribe Pakistani Customs officials to smooth the way for exporting rugs to Germany and the US. At times he took his Uncle's place in Peshawar and watched the looms, which eventually numbered about 280. Of course by this time none of the family-members was weaving rugs. They were important producers of carpets for export to America and Europe, and they also produced carpets for other Afghans who then sold them to their own customers. Their business was well established by the time the huge numbers of Afghans of all stripes poured out of Afghanistan in the 1980s, all of them looking for work and for help. The family gave both work and help to as many as they could.

But, gradually, Khalil's father became aware of a problem with the family business. Virtually all Turkmen refugees wove red and blue rugs with repeating octagonal medallions. There was nothing to distinguish the family's rugs from everyone else's. He wondered whether there were other designs that might set his rugs apart and give them a competitive edge. And so it was that Father sent the 20 year old Khalil to America with, first of all, the near-fatal instruction to try to fit in and not be conspicuous when he reached America, and then, once there, to identify new designs and colors that would sell well in that famously wealthy country. And that is when Khalil landed in Venice Beach, California and learned to fit in. He learned to wear gold chains and tiny bathing suits and to snort cocaine.

A year later his father showed up in Venice Beach and took him firmly by his Western-style collar and the seat of his britches and led him into a 12-step program. But by then Khalil had met an American woman who taught him the facts of life. Sitting together one night in the balmy pool-side night air of Southern California, they watched the stars and she began to talk about them. She told him about the Big Bang. She said that he and she were looking at the stars as they had been millions of years ago and not as they were now, and she explained about the speed of light. She told him about evolution and suggested that it was random mutations that guided the human drama rather than the hand of God. She insisted that human embryos at a certain stage had gill slits. She told him that each fertilized human egg had within it a complete blueprint of what it would become. In one long talk under the stars, she passed on to him the wisdom of Western civilization and he bought all of it.

So when his Father came to reclaim him, it was already too late, for by then he considered himself an American, and he could no longer imagine leading a Turkmen life of God and family and rugs. He overcame his drug addiction but stayed put in California and married the woman who had taught him the facts of life, and in nothing flat (it seemed to him) he owned a restaurant in Little Kabul and had a beautiful seven-year-old daughter who belted out *Somewhere Over the Rainbow* in front of strangers.

And then Avery Deane sat him down in front of a loom and gave him good money—or, rather, was *going* to pay him good money upon completion—to weave a rug, and for three weeks Khalil had been fixed by the fierce and humorous eyes of a dragon that seemed to ask, "Who are you? Do you travel in disguise?" With each knot he tied and with each flick of his knife as he cut the yarn, Khalil began to find his old rhythm at the loom, and, as he did, he began to think that he had begun to make a turn in his life's journey, and that someday he would have come full circle.

Chapter Nineteen

He kept glancing over at the black and tan Silver Cloud, and then he stopped talking and gazed at it as if he had never seen it before. "God!" he said. "What a splendid automobile."

 "My God, Holden, you're wasting away in this dusty little store! Lock it up! We're going to Napa Valley. All aboard!" On his last two words, Avery Deane's voice pitched upward to a thrilling howl. With his voice alone, his golden pipes, Dean could have led all of the children out of the village, like the Pied Piper of Hamlin. Even now as he entered Holden's rug store, Deane led a small retinue: Sandra and Khalil. "Let's go pick up Laura!" Deane said. He meant the journalist Holden was dating.

Holden loved the thought of spending a day in Napa Valley with Laura. "Is there room?"

"Of course there is. We're taking your car."

"Where's your Porsche?"

"I'm in the market for a new car. You can help me buy one in Napa. Come on lad, let's go!"

By now Holden had nearly come to terms with closing shop in the middle of the day and running off on whatever adventure Deane roped him into. He had signs to hang on the door for every contingency: Back by 2 PM, Closed for the

Day, Closed Due to Illness and so on. It was strange, he thought, but even though he missed a day of work now and then doing Deane's bidding, sales had never been so good. At Deane's urging he had raised all of his prices, and sales increased. He had even been thinking he should hold back some of his best pieces, and of course they went flying off the walls. These days, if he took four hours off work, customers were waiting to get in. He knew that Deane had everything to do with his sudden success and so could not refuse him when he said, "Let's go!" Nor could he bring himself to raise hell with him about the silk Kirman that had never materialized, nor to demand his money back.

After a phone call to Laura, Holden put up his "Gone all Day" sign, locked his door and drove off to pick her up, with Dean, Khalil and Sandra in the back seat. Ten minutes later, Laura answered her door, ready to go, her hair styled short and snappy. "Hi all," she said to those in the car. "I'm Laura."

Dean first directed Holden to an address in St. Helena where he said there was an automobile he wanted to see. "And Holden, my friend, it's not a sniveling little Toy*ota*. You'll see." And it wasn't. It was a 1971 Rolls Royce Silver Cloud. Its owner proudly presented it on his estate's grass-lined, winding driveway. Holden and the others were impressed by the splendid old car, but Deane was visibly moved by it. The car's owner, a retired judge named Henry Baron, watched as Avery Dean approached the old two-toned beauty as if it were royalty. He walked around it slowly, quietly, and when he finally touched it, he first pulled out his handkerchief and used it like a white glove, sparing the car's finish the indignity of being touched by the human hand. His expression was that of an art lover before a de Vinci. A few minutes later he turned to Judge Barron and took his hand in both of his, clearly startling the old man.

"Don't sell it, sir."

"What's that?"

Dean narrowed his eyes and whispered, "Keep it. Don't sell it. I'll find another automobile to buy, but you, sir...you'll never forgive yourself if you sell it." The owner looked confused. For one thing, he seemed to be trying to get his hand back from Deane, who not only had his hand but was also standing much too close. At the same time he was obviously pleased that Deane liked his Rolls Royce.

"Well, 'keep it.' Of course. That's what I think, too. But the wife, you know. She's the practical one. Insurance and all that. Yes, I'd love to keep it." Holden thought that the old judge really was having second thoughts. He kept glancing over at the black and tan Silver Cloud, and then he stopped talking and gazed at it as if he had never seen it before. "God!" he said. "What a splendid automobile."

Deane dropped his hand but then took his arm and led him closer to the automobile. "Sir, look at its finish. Only time and good care can build such a deep glow. And the leather. Saddle soap and love. Saddle soap and love. It shows, sir. There's no substitute. Don't sell it."

"God!"

"My friends and I will just excuse ourselves and leave you here with your Rolls. Thank you. Thank you. I'm moved." Deane shook the man's hand again and backed away from him and the car as if unwilling to turn his back to them. Holden and the others started back to the Toyota, but the car's owner seemed to break out of his spell.

"But wait," he called to Deane. "Maybe you'd better drive it or something. Take it around, see how it runs. I mean, I'm just thinking of the wife."

Dean stopped backing away but said nothing.

"Don't you want to know how much I'm asking for it?"

"Money?" Dean said. "That's not it. I'm sure you'd ask something fair if you were to let it go, but sir..." Dean shook his head.

"Well, take it out and drive it. Take your friends around. Visit a winery, have some fun. Then come on back and we'll talk about it."

Deane looked serious. Finally he started back toward the Rolls Royce and its owner until he again stood a little too close. He took his hand. "I would be honored, sir. Honored."

Next, Deane and his retinue went shopping for Napa Valley property. "No less than 60 acres," he explained to a realtor.

"Planted or unplanted?"

"Planted. Old-vine Cabernet, and let's take my car." Somehow they all fit into the Rolls Royce.

"Where are you from?" the realtor asked Deane in a friendly voice from the back seat.

" *Here*....now: the gorgeous Napa Valley." It *was* gorgeous. Not spectacular but peaceful, open, friendly, warm and, at the valley's limits where mountains rose, rolling. Deane drove where the realtor directed and finally passed through a stone gate and then down a dirt road lined by old olive trees that met overhead. He pulled aside to let a tractor lumber slowly around them. Deane and his passengers waved at the farmer who raised a finger to them without smiling. Deane eased the Rolls Royce back onto the dirt lane. All around them grape vines with gnarly old trunks wrapped around simple trellises and leaned toward the sun.

Gradually a Victorian farmhouse revealed itself at the end of the road and Deane slowed even further. The vineyards grew right up to the house on both of its sides with no yard or fence between them. The house and the vines looked as if they had sprung from the same soil and were ruled by the same sun and rain. Railroad ties in front of the house marked parking places, and the Silver Cloud rolled to a slow stop. Holden, in the back seat with Laura and the realtor, felt shy about breaking the peace and he waited in the car, peering at the house. So did the others until finally the realtor got out. Then everyone stepped out of the car and stretched and gazed at the house and the apple trees and peach trees that surrounded the front of the home and at the mountains that were not so far off.

Even the realtor hung back from the front door, perhaps waiting for someone to greet them. "I called," he said. "He's expecting us." He and the others looked around when they noticed the tractor they had seen a moment ago lumbering along toward them. The farmer pulled up by the group, letting its engine run.

"One of you wants to farm 80 acres?" The old man looked on them with suspecting eyes.

"That would be Mr. Deane here," the realtor said, presenting his client. "You must be Clem Briano."

The farmer glowered. "That's some fancy car you've got there, feller." He and Deane eyed each other. Holden watched them both, uncomfortable.

Finally Deane said, "I'll trade you straight across for your tractor." The farmer might have been amused. Holden couldn't tell.

"Nope."

"Okay, I'll trade you this car for all your peach trees."

"Nope."

"Well then, how about for all your peaches?"

"Nope."

"Well what about for just one peach?" The farmer did smile a little.

"Nope."

"Then it looks like my car isn't worth much out here."

"Not to me."

Deane looked at him. "You ever look under the hood of one of these? Because it's pretty interesting." He went to the Silver Cloud and popped the hood and raised it while the farmer watched. After a while the farmer pushed his throttle and the engine of his tractor revved down. He dismounted and sauntered over to the Rolls where he and Deane together gazed at its engine and got to talking about this and that.

After that the farmer, Clem, led them around the vineyard. "This here's cabernet sauvignon grapes. That's all I grow." Holden thought Deane would tell the old farmer to lock them up, but he was unusually quiet.

"They look a hundred years old," Deane said.

"Ninety."

"Yep."

Holden wondered whether he had heard right. Did Avery really say 'Yep?' He noticed that Deane handled every piece of equipment that the farmer called to his attention. He smelled every rose bush. He tasted the apples and peaches off the trees. He knelt and picked up a handful of soil here and there and smelled it. He sat on the tractor and started the engine and lifted the front end loader. He examined the vines and the grapes that were beginning to color. Inside the Victorian house, he patted the fine old stove and ran his hand along the curved banister of the staircase. He looked out of an upstairs window at the vineyards surrounding the property. And he kept his lip zipped.

Finally they all gathered back at the Rolls Royce. "Well, what do you think, fella?" the farmer asked Deane. The realtor kept back, knowing it was up to them. Sandra and Khalil and Laura and Holden hung back with him and watched.

"I think you'd better keep it, don't you?"

He considered. "I'm getting too damn old to work it."

"Would you like to stay?"

"Yep."

Holden wondered, "Did he learn that from Deane or was it the other way around?"

"Well why don't you spin off about 20 acres and give it to some young family in exchange for working the whole farm for the next 10 or 20 years? They don't have to live here unless you want them to."

"Well, 10 or 20 years would sure do the trick, wouldn't it?" The farmer smiled a little and then thought for a while. "I could do that. I never thought of it before."

"You want to?"

"Yeah."

"Well then it's about time we were on our way." Everyone began climbing back into the Silver Cloud, waving goodbye to the farmer and saying what a nice place he had here.

When Dean was back behind the wheel, the old man came to his window and took his shoulder. "Will you all come back and visit?" he asked.

Holden didn't know exactly what had happened. Finally he said to Deane, "Do you really want to buy a vineyard?" Deane didn't answer. "You didn't have much to say to the old fellow."

"I was listening to him talk. Did you hear his voice? And his dialect? They're wonderful! God!"

When they drove down the lawn-bordered driveway near St. Helena where Deane had picked up the Rolls Royce, Judge Barron came out and asked Deane, "How did you like it?"

Avery Deane asked, "What did your wife say?"

He grinned. "She said I could keep it."

The friends broke out in a cheer. Deane out shouted them all, though.

"Then drive it man! Don't sell it!"

A few minutes later they were back in Holden's old Toyota, on their way home. It had been a long day, but everyone was in a good mood.

Chapter Twenty

"By the time you're finished, I want you to know how the Ferrier Dragon Rug smells."

 Sarah held the phone away from her ear as Ulysses Pope shouted. "Well where the hell is it? China? Here? Does it exist at all?"

"I don't know, Ulysses." Sarah Atwood was one of the few people who could call the old billionaire rug collector by his first name. "All he told me is that the prospects for getting it are looking better and that he should know more in a month or so."

"Well if I have to come up with a million dollars in a month or two, I have to know more than that! Has he seen it?"

"No. He says a friend in China thinks it's the real thing. He says that his friend has connections with the Chinese military, and evidently the military controls Chinese antiquities. This fellow is trying to get it out of the country right now."

"The Ferrier Dragon Rug?"

"That's what he says."

The old man was silent for a moment. "Well, don't scare him off. Tell him I've got the money. Don't tell him my name, though."

"Of course not," but she thought, "You old fool. Who do you think you're kidding? Who else has $1,000,000 to buy a 4 by 5 foot rug?" Out loud she said, "So anyway, I thought I should inform you."

"Call me day or night! Day or night. I *want* that rug!"

"I'll keep you posted, Ulysses. Don't worry, I'll keep you posted."

"I'm *not* worried! Just get me that rug."

"Of course."

"Day or night."

"Yes, day or night."

"He's worried," she thought. "Good."

"You think this guy is on the up-and-up? A million dollars is enough to bring crooks out of the woodwork."

Sarah had to laugh, but she kept it to herself. "A million dollars?" she thought. "Stick *that* much money under our noses and aren't we all crooks?" But to Pope she said, "I don't know, Ulysses. This man is strange. Queen's English. Refined manners. Breeding. He's a wound-up sort, though. On the edge."

"On the edge of what? What are you talking about?"

It took her a while to answer as she thought back on her encounter with Deane in the Museum. "Well, on the edge of sanity." She laughed out loud. "On the edge of good-looking, too. Little man, big voice. Big, beautiful voice. Energy, charisma. He said he and I don't care about money. I believed him. At least I believed it about *him*."

"I still don't know what the hell you're talking about. God damn it, Sarah, just get me that rug."

"It's best if you don't hold your breath, Ulysses. It'll either happen or it won't. It probably won't." Sarah wondered why it amused her to tease Pope. Maybe Deane *was* a crook or a con man, but, still, he was her best hope for getting the Ferrier Dragon Rug for Pope and a $100,000 commission for herself—or at least coming up with a rug that might *pass* for the Ferrier rug.

Ulysses Pope grumbled and hung up.

The truth is that Sarah had become impatient with the course she had chosen—the "rug path," she called it. She had chosen it in cold blood, without being the least bit interested in Oriental rugs, and she had done so because of the opportunities the rug world seemed to offer for making a killing. In nothing flat she had risen to the pinnacle: curator of one of the most important museum collections of rugs in the country, where she trafficked in rugs worth millions of dollars. Thus far, none of those millions had rubbed off onto her.

Rather than being so cynical, she thought, perhaps she should have found a profession that involved something she loved...and the money would have followed. What did she love, though? Money.

Really, after 6 years of climbing the ladder, her best chance for some decent money was that Avery Deane would come up with the Ferrier Dragon Rug. With all her hopes vested in him, she had begun to remember him as larger than life. Of course he wasn't literally large. He was rather short. But she remembered how he seemed to wake up the museum as she had guided him through her part of it: shouting, purring, imploring her to "Lock 'em up!" Who*ever* he was. She didn't know where he was from, even. Who did he know? Who knew him? She had seen him at Ulysses Pope's boring talk in Berkeley where Pope had been trying to drum up members for his rug society. Deane must have been invited by that rug dealer what's his name. Holden Caufield. Holden something. Maybe the rug dealer knew more about him. She thought she might call Holden and see if she could find out more about Avery Deane. If she could remember his last name. Holden...Holden something.

A short while after Ulysses Pope grumbled and hung up on Sarah, Marley Phillips received a phone call from the old rug mogul.

"Listen here, Phillips, I'm going to tell you something and I want you to keep your mouth shut about it."

Ah, Phillips thought, there's no one quite like Ulysses Pope. Thank God. Aloud he said, "Of course, Mr. Pope."

"I might be able to put my hands on the old Ferrier Dragon Rug. Do you know anything about it?"

Phillips was stunned. "You're kidding!"

"Phillips, have you ever known me to kid? Don't be an ass."

"Uh...It's just that I always thought the Ferrier rug probably was a myth. It's real? You know where it is?"

"I told you, I *might*."

"Well that's marvelous! I don't know what to say!"

"Don't say a damned thing to anybody. Is that clear?"

"Of course."

"Before I acquire this rug I want to make very certain that it's the real thing. That's where you come in. Phillips, I want you to become the world's expert on the rug. Read everything that has ever been written about it. Then, when the time comes, I want you to authenticate it for me. Got that?"

Phillips thought for a moment. "What you're asking is impossible. How can I authenticate something that no one has ever seen? All we have is a written description."

"Damn it, don't argue with me! If you're worth your salt you will be able to tell me whether the rug is *old* enough. You'll be able to tell me whether its *weave* makes sense. You'll know whether it matches Ferrier's *description*. Just tell me whether you want the job or not. If I get the rug, I'll pay you $10,000 to examine it and tell me whether it's the Ferrier rug."

"Mr. Pope, Charles Evans Green could do the same thing, and he probably wouldn't charge for the advice."

"The difference between him and you is that you'll know if the rug is a forgery and he won't. Also, I'll want you to be on the scene within a few hours of the time I get my hands on the rug. It probably will land on the West Coast."

"From where?"

"None of your business."

"Provided by whom?"

"None of your business."

"Maybe it is. I am aware of at least one man capable of making quite good fakes. Would you describe the person who might bring you the rug?"

"I don't know what he looks like. I just know a bunch of nonsense about him. He's on the edge, whatever that means. Speaks the Queen's English. Small man, big voice. Charismatic. A bunch of nonsense."

"Hmm. And if you don't manage to get the rug for me to examine?"

"I'll pay you $5000 anyway. Plus expenses."

"All right. I'll start my research tonight."

"Good. By the time you're finished, I want you to know how the Ferrier Dragon Rug *smells*."

"Well, I'll know whether this rug smells fishy or not."

"That's why we have you, Phillips. You have a good nose." Phillips had to agree. He had a good nose for fakes.

"Small man, big voice." The timing of Pope's phone call was strange. Since Phillips had taught his graduate seminar on archeological fakes several weeks ago, he had been thinking again about the two rugs in the National Carpet Museum's collection that he knew were forgeries. He had never discovered who had faked them, but he did have a suspect in mind, the fellow of mysterious origins and unknown name whom several New York rug dealers had fingered as the most likely perpetrator, someone they had without exception called a small man with a big voice. And now Marley had just received a phone call from Ulysses Pope that set off bells.

Of course he didn't know whether the rug that Pope was expecting to get was a fake or not. Maybe it was the real thing. But Phillips thought that already he was catching a whiff of rat. The rug was going to surface on the West Coast? Maybe he should research it there, and, while he was at it, he might just ask around rug-circles about a short rug guy with a big voice. He thought he might start in San Francisco. And, of course, Berkeley.

Chapter Twenty-One

"Though river gunk adorns it, do not fear."

The day came when Khalil arose from his work, stretched, and then began to snip away the threads that held his finished rug to the loom. As it fell to the floor, it seemed to Avery Deane less like a wooly picture in a frame and more like a rug. Relieved and moved, he improvised a boisterous song to the tune of an old English madrigal:

"I think you're going to like it Sarah dear.
I know you're going to love it, do not fear."

After months of work, the rug was off the loom and it looked wonderful! Of course he saw it with a father's eye. The average observer would have thought the rug a thick and tangled mess, for its unclipped pile was an inch long, like a shag rug, and its design was garbled and indistinct. But he broke out again in song:

"The rug will be a work of art,
Our dandy dragon melt your heart,
I know you're going to love it, Sarah dear."

"Who's Sarah?" Khalil asked.

"Ah, Sarah! It's she for whom we're making this wonderful rug, my friend. The lovely Sarah."

"Are you going to *give* it to her?"

That caught Deane. Give it to her? It *was* a shame that money had to enter into this. But soon he had to settle with Khalil for his three months of weaving, and Cherise for dyeing the wool and with Kadija, Zainab, Soroya and Fatima for their spinning. And there was his rent, of course, which he had not paid in some time, bless Sandra's heart. And he would have to replace his Porsche. He still owed Holden for the silk Kirman. And he owed that fellow Bob for the same Kirman. There were other debts, too, that he would rather not think about. It was astonishing how petty some people could be where debts were concerned. So he would have to sell the dragon rug. But he was confident that it would make Sarah happy nonetheless. But he *would* like to give it to her. Maybe he would.

I'll give to you my treasure Sarah dear,
Though a dragon guards it, Sarah, do not fear.
The rug will be your guiding star,
Its air of wisdom lead you far,
I know you're going to love it Sarah dear.

How good it was to be alive! Deane watched as Khalil laid the rug flat on the floor and began to shorten and even-out its pile with a tool he had brought from Afghanistan, a tool designed in central Asia four thousand years ago for the sole purpose of clipping the pile of an Oriental rug. It was like a scissor whose blades were turned sideways to its handle, and with it Khalil cut off the top half of the shaggy pile so that soon it was an amazingly uniform half-inch throughout. Each clip of the scissor revealed a curling dragon tail or a flaming pearl, a wave, a dragon's eye.

"You know, that dragon's eyes kept me awake every night, boss," Khalil said as he worked. It seemed to Deane that Khalil tried not to look at the dragon even as his clipping gave it focus. "I used to dream that it asked me, 'What are you doing here, Khalil? Why aren't you back home taking care of your parents.' Things like that."

"No, the dragon was saying, 'Khalil Zadeh is the best cook in all the land and the best rug-weaver, too. Khalil belongs *here* and the people of Fremont, California hope he stays forever.' The dragon is saying, 'Your wife and daughter love you and are happy you are here taking care of them and there are many people back home to take care of your parents.'"

Khalil laughed. "I didn't hear it say that.."

"That's why this rug is so good, Khalil. It's magic." To Deane it seemed as if Khalil had half-again more teeth than the average person and that they all showed when he smiled.

Finally Avery Deane was alone with the clipped rug, and he stood back, regarding it, still humming. He saw just what he had expected to see and had hoped to see: A rug of extraordinary interest and beauty—and it was brand new. Though expected, its newness was daunting. Somehow it would have to become a 350-year-old rug in a month, give or take. "And that's where the magic comes in," he said aloud. "That's why we have *me*."

The next day he put on his beret and silk scarf and took a bus to a store in Berkeley that rented tools. On the bus he noticed once again that his fellow humans were sadly lacking in style, manners and hygiene. Though he found them distasteful, still his heart went out to them. Poor blokes. He couldn't resist trying to help one fellow. "For God's sake, man, look at your shoes!" The man seemed startled and deeply concerned, and of course he looked down at his shoes. So did everyone else within ear-shot of Deane's powerful voice. "Why, what color are they? One can't make it out, they're so scuffed! Now what kind of impression do you hope to make with shoes like that?" The fellow looked around as if for a way out. Others on the bus maintained blank faces as they followed the action, looking first at the fellow's shoes, then at Deane, then to the poor fellow to see what he was going to do, and finally back to his shoes. Deane went on, "You know, shoe polish only costs a few cents. Practically nothing! Three minutes to apply! Appearances matter! That's why I drive a Porsche." But Deane could see that the man was too far gone to follow his reasoning. "Well," he thought, "You can lead a horse to water..." He decided to let it go. After a while, the fellow with the scuffed shoes walked to the door at the back of the bus and acted like his stop was coming right up and he was getting ready to leave, but Deane thought he was just avoiding coming to terms with the poor choices he had made in life.

Back home, Deane went to work on the dragon rug with his rented tools. First, the belt sander. He revved it up and held the sander just above the rug and began to wag it in the air as some people wave their fountain pen above a document before signing their name, waiting for inspiration, waiting till he sensed just where to lower it onto the rug's colorful pile. He half-closed his eyes and, like an artist—no, as an artist—he dropped the sander onto the rug and let the sander spin. Atomized fragments of wool filled the air, and soon a pattern of wear emerged on the rug's surface, especially around its edges and dead in its center. Anyone not knowing how the wear had come to exist would have wondered how the rug had been used. There was something about the wear that suggested ritual use, an impression that was heightened by the fiery dragon. Had temple lanterns had been placed around the rug's perimeter for many years, or bones of ancestors had been tossed onto it in some pagan rite? And the low spot right in its center- had a small, carved deity or other ritual object presided there for decades? Anyway, most people would now have assumed that the rug was old, though it would have been hard to say whether it was 30 years old or much older. In fact, the rug was anomalous and therefore disturbing—even Deane felt uneasy—because somehow it now looked both new and old at the same time.

Finished with his belt sander, he fired up his rental blowtorch. Luckily, Deane had previous blowtorch experience, having tamed a number of his previous creations with one—two of which were now mounted on a wall in the San Francisco Museum and labeled "Mid-19th century"—so he knew just how to regulate the torch's impressive flame. He started by torching the rug's back, burning off all the fuzz that one finds on the backs of new rugs. Next he singed all the new-rug fuzz off the rug's front side, making sure that the torch did not linger too long in any one place, then extinguished the torch's flame and swept the smoldering rug on both sides with a stiff brush. Even after Deane carefully brushed away all the charred wool from its surface, a subtle dark patina clung to the rug, along with the odor of burnt sheep. "Now," Deane thought, "we're getting somewhere." Suddenly it looked a hundred years old, "which," he continued, "isn't at all old enough." Furthermore, he noted, though it now looked reasonably old, it didn't feel old. It still had the stiff handle of a new rug. There was much more work to do.

Of course he knew that in the Middle East the stiffness of new rugs was usually conquered by placing them on busy streets to be run over by automobiles. In more rural areas herds of sheep or camels served the purpose. In recent decades chemicals sometimes were used to turn a stiff new rug into a floppy old thing in a matter of hours, but Deane was unwilling to risk spoiling the dragon rug with chemicals—nor did he want trace amounts of a chemical to be found in his rug if it were carefully scrutinized. On the other hand, he had neither a herd of sheep nor even an automobile with which to soften it up. He sat down, humming, and thought. He couldn't very well spread the rug in a city street or a freeway. In Afghanistan motorists knew the game, but, here, motorists would swerve to avoid running over a rug in the street. Tumble it in a clothes dryer? Not powerful enough. What would he do? Suddenly he thought of the answer and he sighed. What a lot of work. In the remaining hours of daylight, he laid the rug out on the concrete driveway near the rear of the apartment building and began to smash it with a hammer, inch by inch. *Pow! Pow! Pow!* In two hours the rug was as floppy as a blanket, and there was no longer even a hint of newness about it.

Sanded, singed and hammered, it looked like something on which four generation of children had been raised. But it did not look three or four centuries old. There was still more to do.

The next morning Deane tucked the rug under one arm and carried a small garden spade with the other and headed for the Berkeley hills in an AC Transit bus: First to north Berkeley, then up steep Marin Avenue, then off to the left onto Spruce, then finally to Spruce and Grizzly Peak where he disembarked. From there he headed on foot down into Tilden Park, a territory he was familiar with from the days when, sleeping completely recumbent in the driver's seat of his Porsche 928, he had called it home. As he hiked, he sometimes caught a whiff of burned wool that wafted from the rug under his arm. Except for that, the spring air was delicious.

At a campground called Eucalyptus Grove he left the road and dropped down to a trail that ran along Tilden Creek. A half mile up the creek, bay trees that were rooted at the creek's edge leaned into the trail and narrowed it, making it hard for Deane to keep going. He draped the would-be million dollar dragon rug over his neck the way he normally would have worn a scarf, used the shovel as a walking stick and scrambled through brush until he felt that he was well away from the normal pack of weekend hikers. Breathing hard, he looked around carefully, and when he was convinced he was alone, he descended the steep bank to the creek's edge. He easily jumped the creek and found a dense thicket of brush to duck behind, and there he began digging in the soil about four feet away from the creek. The clayey soil was just right—*slightly* damp—and he dug a little ditch about five feet long and a foot deep. That done, he took another close look around and then opened the dragon rug and spread it on the ground as well as he was able. For a moment he gazed at it, startled by its beauty. The dragon he had created seemed to float on its surface, bristling, staring at him, challenging. For a moment he peered into the dragon's eyes. High overhead a raptor *screeed* and broke the spell. Deane shoveled about half of the damp soil he had taken from the ditch onto the rug's surface, spread it with his spade as evenly as he could and rolled up the rug with the clay inside. He laid it in the ditch and, finally, backfilled the ditch till the rug was buried. He pulled brush onto the scar in the ground, gathered his bearings, marked the trail inconspicuously with rocks and headed back toward Eucalyptus Grove and home. And as he walked he began to hum and then to sing aloud.

"I know you're going to love it, Sarah dear,
Though river gunk adorns it, do not fear.
The rug will be a work of art,
Our dandy dragon melt your heart,
I know you're going to love it, Sarah dear."

Chapter Twenty-Two

"King of my castle," he said aloud, "but you do
have to defend it, don't you?"

 During the past several months, the summer months, Holden had been in a sunnier mood. Rarely now did he peer glumly down the Black Hole of Calcutta. He wondered what had brought on the change. Did his ascent out of gloom begin when thirty people dropped out of the Ali Babba Society on his behalf? During his three years in business, he had believed himself to be invisible in the rug world, but when Pope had embarrassed him, his colleagues and customers had all stood up for him. Maybe that's when his mood had begun to change.

Or had it been even earlier, when Avery Deane had shown up in his store, crabby and loud and exciting, shouting like a mad man, "Lock 'em up!" Holden had felt *discovered*. Or, rather, his rugs had been discovered and respected. Suddenly here was someone else who seemed to value them as highly as Holden. In fact, Deane may have valued them even more than Holden. "You're giving them away, man. You're *giving* them away!" And suddenly Holden had found their beauty and importance again. Maybe that's when his mood began to change, when Avery Deane walked through the door. Holden thought so.

But, goodness knows, there was a price to be paid, too, as he was reminded when Deane walked through the door that morning as he had done so often.

Holden was glad to see him, despite everything. Despite everything? Well, Deane could be a problem. For instance, not all of Holden's customers enjoyed having a man shout at them such things as, "It's not a sniveling little Chevy, man, it's a Mercedes! A Mer*cedes*!" Some folks who entered the rug store believed that Deane was a mad man, plain and simple, and, frightened, they got the hell out. And others felt that there were some very hard-sale tactics going on here, and they left too. And, furthermore, Holden did not enjoy the fact that many of his customers assumed that Deane was the shop's owner and that Holden worked for him. So having Deane in the store was a mixed bag. Very.

And he could be grouchy and irritable. With Dean, you could never tell.

That morning he had come in singing some song Holden wasn't familiar with. He spun about the shop looking at Holden's new acquisitions, praising them, urging him to raise his prices even higher, though Holden had already marked them up considerably. A customer came in, then another. Just as Deane was getting ready to grab one of them by an elbow, another man walked through the door and stopped dead in his tracks when he saw Avery Deane. The man had the look of a boxer. Was it his broken nose? His epicanthic fold? His forward-thrusting head? Or his loud voice?

"Well, speak of the devil! Old Jake himself." (Had he heard right, Holden wondered. Jake? Is that what the prizefighter had called Deane? Because obviously he was talking to Deane.) Deane checked him out and then ignored the fellow.) "Just the bloke I was hoping to run into someday." The man was loud and aggressive, and Holden and his customers glanced at him nervously.

"Uh, can I help you?" Holden asked.

"*He* can." The man pointed at Deane. "He can help me by paying off his bloody debts." Holden had the sensation that this wasn't really happening, a sensation that was added to by the man's accent. He could have been Avery's brother. He spoke just like him, though without the gorgeous, soaring voice. But brotherhood seemed unlikely. While Deane was less than 5'7", this man was a burly 6'2." Deane ignored him and turned the corner of a rug mounted on the wall to examine its back, but he had quit humming. The big guy lumbered up behind Deane and put a big hand on his shoulder. "I guess you don't recognize me, huh Jake?" His voice dripped stupid sarcasm. One of the customers hurried out the door. Holden was very unhappy.

Deane turned and brushed the man's hand off his shoulder and faced him. "Ever the gentleman, yes Johnson? Still a bit heavy of jowl, I see, and a little heavy handed. If you have something to ask me you can ask politely."

"I don't have to be overly polite, now do I, when I'm asking for something that is mine to begin with? Where's my money, that's what I'm asking?"

"I have invested it for you, Johnson. Now if you will quit acting like a goon you will have your money twice over."

The "goon" stuck out his broad hand for his money, and squared his jaw and shoulders at Deane. The one remaining customer moved closer to the door.

Holden had to do something. "Look, gentlemen, let's keep this polite and let's keep it quiet. This is a place of business."

"Better not get involved with this one, mate," Johnson said to Holden, though he still stared at Deane and held out his hand. "He'll take you to the cleaners. Next it will be *you* trying to get your money from this big-mouth." Holden shuddered. Deane still owed him for the silk Kirman. Just then Deane slapped Johnson's hand away and began roaring.

"You bloody fucking idiot! Go back to your cave and scratch yourself. And get out of my face!" Johnson lunged, but Deane slipped him like a bullfighter and Johnson crashed into a rug on the wall. The last customer dashed out the door. Deane twirled around the showroom like a dervish while the boxer tried to catch him. Deane goaded, "If you were a lot smarter, Johnson, you'd be a moron." Johnson growled as he lunged again and again.

Now, in the last few years Holden had been through a lot. He had been shunned by no less than Marley Phillips, Sarah Atwood, Charles Evans Green, Ulysses Pope and Kyle Berman in one evening in Washington, D.C. He had suffered the long, slow, retailer's death of no sales for most of three years. He had been made a monkey of by Ulysses Pope. He had stood by while customers assumed that Deane owned the store and that Holden worked for him. But he had never had to watch a couple of madmen drive away his customers. With unambiguous clarity, suddenly he understood that it was *his* shop, *his* castle, his livelihood, his stand to make. As people sometimes explain after flying far outside their normal bounds, "something snapped." Before he had time to be afraid or to think this through or to put a sign in his window saying "Closed for Fistfight," he dashed between the dervish and the caveman, threw his arms out and yelled his head off. "OUT! OUT! BOTH OF YOU! OUT OF MY STORE!" Hyperventilating but unstoppable, he shouted, "I'm going to count to three and if you guys are still here, I'm going to take your arms off." He dropped his doubled-up fists to his hips and gazed first into Deane's eyes and then Johnson's, challenging them both. "One," he said. They stopped.

"Two."

Deane laughed. "Go Holden! Throw us out!" Holden glared at him, then at Johnson.

"Three. All right!" And that's when he pretty much went berserk, though he didn't seriously hurt anybody. And in the end Deane and Johnson were outside on the sidewalk and he was standing in his doorway, dusting his hands off. The two outside had grins on their faces, maybe sheepish grins or maybe amused grins.

The big one said to the other, "That's the nicest place we've ever been thrown out of."

Deane explained, "That's my boy Holden. He's a good man."

Holden slammed the door and then turned and leaned back against it. For a while he could hear them outside, first laughing, then arguing; laughing again and walking away. He smiled.

"King of my castle," he said aloud, "but you do have to defend it, don't you?" It was a rhetorical question. In fact he had defended his castle, and that didn't hurt Holden's sunny mood at all.

There was no end to his surprises that day. Not long after he tossed Deane and Johnson out of his store, a very tall man walked in whom Holden instantly recognized as Marley Phillips. Even as he welcomed him to his store and shook his hand, he remembered the hour he had spent in Phillips's company—and in the company of Ulysses Pope, Kyle Berman, Charles Evans Green and Sarah Atwood. They had completely ignored him, as if, like the magnificent Serapi the rug moguls had stood on, he were invisible. So now, as he shook hands, Holden held a little of his usual goodwill in reserve.

Phillips clearly didn't remember him. He made a cursory tour around the store and praised a rug or two. He made another round and looked closer at a couple of the rugs and stopped praising them. Then he stopped looking at them, or, rather, he glanced at them surreptitiously, from the corner of his eye. He asked about a couple of pieces that, Holden knew, had no particular merit. He began to make small talk: weather and things like that.

After watching Deane sell dozens of rugs in his store, Holden understood that collectors believe that expressing an interest in a carpet will drive its price up, and so they are forced to find a way to both ignore it and to buy it. Usually they mention it casually, like, "Hey, look at that Salor. One end is quite a bit wider than the other, isn't it? I wonder what its weaver was smoking. Hah, hah, hah!"

Holden had learned to ignore this first thrust. That forced the collector to try again. Often their second stab involved damning with faint praise, like, "It *is* a decent Salor, though. Too bad about its dyes." Of course there was more going on than a collector trying to keep a rug's price from going up.

Actually, they were hoping to drive it *down*. In any case, Holden knew that at that point it was safe to enter into an academic discussion of the rug. For instance he might agree that it probably *was* a Salor, though it was hard to be certain, considering its rarity. And so the dance proceeded, with neither the buyer nor seller seemingly able to stop the music.

He was sure that Phillips's apparent indifference was a sign that he was interested in one of Holden's rugs. Phillips confirmed it a moment later when he said casually, "You know, I disagree with your attribution on that rug you're calling a Kazak. I believe it's a Karabaugh." In effect, Marley Phillips the third had speeded up the dance, cutting right to the good-natured-academic-discussion stage.

But Holden was in a strange mood. Having recently taken the measure of two famous rug figures—Ulysses Pope and Sarah Atwood—and having finally become clear that they were sorry excuses for humankind, he found himself under-whelmed by the presence of yet another. And then, too, he had just thrown two grown men out of his store and had established what had not been so clear before, namely that he was the owner of his rug store and that, in it, he didn't have to dance to anyone's music but his own. So instead of arguing about the provenance of his rug—and it *was* his—and engaging in a dance that had everything to do with Phillips trying to get his price down, he said, "All my rugs have price tags, and my prices are firm." In that instant he hit on a principal from which he never again wavered: that in his store the price was the price, and the price would be the same for Joe Blow, for Ulysses Pope, for Sarah Atwood and everyone else (though not for Laura Scott. He would cheerfully have *given* her anything she wanted.)

But while Holden may have taken pleasure in refusing to dance, Marley Phillips lll was not amused. He was annoyed. "I wasn't talking about the price of the rug. I simply disagree about its provenance." Holden kept quiet, and soon Phillips changed the subject. "Anyway, I wanted to ask you if you've run into a fellow that some people describe as a small man with a big voice? He has a British accent and knows rugs very well."

For some reason, Holden was cautious. "Yes, I think I've run into someone like that. What is his name?"

"Well, it's a funny thing, but I don't really know his name. Do you know it?"

Holden was uncomfortable. "Well, I think I've heard him called Jake."

"Jake?" Holden nodded. He could see that Phillips made a mental note of the name.

"If I see him, shall I tell him you're looking for him?"

"No, no, that's all right. At this stage I just would like to know where he is. But perhaps you could give me a call if you should see him again?"

"Sure," Holden said. "Be glad to."

After Phillips left, Holden wondered what he wanted with Deane, and he also wondered what mischief Deane had been up to. As he pondered, he crumpled up the business card Phillips had given him with his phone number on it and he tossed it in a waste paper basket.

Chapter Twenty-Three

"How are you going to get those worms out of your rug, sir? If you don't mind me asking. And the bugs, too."

A small man with a big voice slipped through the dense branches of bay trees that clogged the trail beside Tilden Creek. When he judged the time right, he began to look for a little pile of rocks by the trail's side and soon he came to it and veered down the creek's bank to where he had buried his rug. This time he didn't bother to carry a spade, for he knew the rug was lying in a shallow ditch covered only with a thin layer of loose soil and brush. He did carry a bag, though—a canvas laundry bag—which he tossed to the ground as he peered up and down the creek and the trail. Satisfied that he was alone, he found what he wanted and began to pull aside sticks and forest duff, and he kicked dirt out of the little ditch. Within seconds the back of the dragon rug was revealed, though it looked more like a filthy old canvas tarp than a rug. In fact Deane was surprised to find that it was quite wet and slimy. When he pulled it out of its shallow grave by one end, it dripped water. Mud and clay clung to it. Deane frowned. He was gripped by a powerful urge to clean his muddy hands. He washed them in the creek and dried them on the laundry bag.

He looked around again and then unrolled it on the damp soil. He had the most peculiar feeling as hundreds of bugs scurried about on the rug, confused and probably blinded by the light. Large black bugs stuck their back ends in the air, threatening to loose a tiny blast of stink. Earthworms tried to burrow into the layer of clay muck that covered the rug. "Bloody *hell!*" he shouted. He startled himself.

Deane looked up. A park ranger stood not ten feet from him, his arms folded, watching. "What are you doing?" the ranger asked.

"What does it bloody hell look like I'm doing?"

"Well, that's what I can't figure. Are you throwing that thing away? Because if you are, that's littering."

"Brilliant! I carried this filthy mess all the way in here to throw it away. You're a regular Sherlock Holmes, I'd say." Deane, who was in a rage, still had the presence to notice that the ranger's expression and the attitude of his body had changed and now suggested a dangerous mix of fear and aggression. The ranger had become afraid that he had cornered a hostile maniac and he reached for his walkie-talkie. Suddenly Deane had an image of being arrested, his rug seized and held as evidence as it rotted into sludge. "Wait, constable, I'll explain. I brought my rug up here to wash in the stream. That's how we always do it in the old country. By far the best way to wash a rug. Natural. Good for it."

"That's a rug?"

"Why yes!" With his shoe, Deane scraped mud from a corner of the rug, and a bit of color showed through the muck. "First we give it a nice mud bath and then we wash it in a river. That's the only way to do it."

Cautiously the ranger drew closer, still holding his walkie-talkie, and he looked at the rug. "Where did you say you come from?"

"I live in Berkeley, your honor. Right here in Berkeley."

"But you said 'In the old country.'"

"Yes, that's how we wash rugs in the old country. Mud bath, then the river. Sometimes we have to do it twice."

"Well we don't do it that way here, sir. Here we call that polluting a stream. You're going to have to take your...rug and leave the park, sir. And don't try to wash it somewhere else in the park. I'll be watching, sir."

"Well, I'm terribly sorry, actually. Hah, hah! Had no idea. Well, I'll just be going on." Deane folded the rug in two and rolled it as the ranger watched.

"How are you going to get those worms out of your rug, sir? If you don't mind me asking. And the bugs, too."

Avery Deane had an impulse to attack the man and beat him to death, but he answered, "Well I suppose I'll have to have it dry cleaned, sheriff. Since I can't wash it in the river." The fellow looked doubtful.

"They might not take it. It's pretty dirty with those worms and everything."

Deane kept working. He stuffed the doubled and rolled rug in his laundry bag. He was sweating. When he was finished he looked at his filthy hands and started for the creek, then stopped and looked at the ranger. The ranger frowned but nodded and then looked away. He did not want to witness the pollution.

Even before the bus came, his bag had begun to leak. Because of that and because of its weight—wet rugs are heavy!—Deane had to drag it behind him. The bus driver eyed it, then focused on Deane, whose face and clothes were splattered with mud. The damp odors of a swamp wafted from Dean and his package. The driver said, "Hey, buddy..." But Deane gave him a steely look, dropped his money in the bin and walked to the back, dragging his bag down the isle, where it left a watery brown trail. Evidently the driver had learned to let some things pass, and he said nothing more to Deane who, in his present mood, probably would have attacked him if he had. On the other hand, his fellow passengers stared at his bag with distaste, even though some were hardly presentable themselves. One very heavy lady with a tiny hat pointedly held her nose. So by the time Deane dragged his bag off of the bus and onto the sidewalk near his apartment building, he was in a towering rage.

He dragged the laundry bag to a hose bib at the rear of the apartment building and he dumped the foul smelling rug out of the bag onto a cement slab, unrolled and then opened it. This time he refused to let the rug's crawly surface paralyze him. He looked at it through half-closed eyes, seeing only enough to work on it. He turned on the water and squirted the rug with the hose. For ten minutes, bugs and muddy brown water ran from it onto the concrete slab, and yet the thick layer of muck that caked the rug's surface never seemed to diminish. "Clay," he said. He laid the hose on the dragon rug and let it run while he went looking for a tool shed. When he found it, he pulled a rake from it, the kind with a rigid spine and teeth. Using the back of the rake, he bore down and squeegeed away mud, clay, worms and small insects that rolled themselves into little balls. Muddy water spread out across the patio.

After twenty minutes of scraping and scrubbing he could see the rug's design and colors, though they were muddied by a deep brown patina, as if the rug had been bathed in Turkish coffee. Deane allowed himself one consoling thought: At least it had not been *eaten* by the bugs that had colonized it. It had no less pile than before he buried it. Still he was not yet ready to focus on it, not yet ready to risk disappointment if the rug were ruined. He turned off the water, left the soggy rug lying in the broken sunlight of a cloudy day and took the back way into the building and into his upstairs apartment where he found a bar of Castile soap. Downstairs again, he unwrapped the soap, knelt and began to rub the bar on the rug's surface, working up a satisfying lather. Then with the back of the rake he worked the suds into the rug's pile and, after ten minutes, turned on the water again and rinsed the rug a second time. Again muddy water poured from it. Finally the water ran clear, and for the first time since he unrolled the rug and began to scrape the muck off its surface, he was willing to risk a real look at it, sans mud, worms and bugs.

As he stood gazing at it, the sun emerged from the clouds and sparkled in the clear water on the rug's surface. Colors danced beneath the water, and a glaring dragon grinned at Deane. Some spirit deep in him soared. He looked away. Just as he had feared to look at the rug when he thought he might have ruined it, now...Was it too good? Too gorgeous? Could *he* have brought it to life? He couldn't look.

"Anyway," he reminded himself, "it's still wet. Maybe it will look terrible when it dries." He gave it a last squeegee to expel all the water he could, then rolled the rug tightly and stood it on end and leaned it against the building so it stayed upright. A few moments later, water began dripping from the end on the concrete. The drying process had begun. As he watched, he began to hum and then to sing.

The next morning he made a phone call. "My dear," he said, "I have something to show you."

Chapter Twenty-Four

Deane laughed his demented laugh. "Art is deception.
Didn't you know that? The better the art,
the better the deception."

 In the still air of a hotel room in Berkeley, Marley Phillips lay back on the stiff bed and prepared himself for battle. Ulysses Pope had commissioned him to become the world's greatest expert on the Ferrier Dragon Rug and to be prepared to authenticate or debunk a rug claiming to be the Ferrier rug that, it was said, would soon surface on the West Coast.

To that end, Phillips had come to Berkeley, not only to be on the West Coast, but because the library at the University of California in Berkeley was known to have a copy of the old Martin book, published in 1908. He had wanted to study the work that had introduced the concept of the Ferrier Rug to the world and which still held the best discussion of it.

It was missing. A library staff-member told him that it had been inventoried in January but had been reported missing by April. There was no record of its having been checked out. Somehow the enormous book—as big as the top of an average-sized coffee table—had been spirited out of the library.

"Who would steal it?" Phillips asked himself as he lay in the gloomy hotel room. But he believed that he knew: A small man with a big voice; someone whom he suspected of having already faked at least two rugs that were now displayed at the National Carpet Museum in Washington, D.C.; someone who had $1,000,000 to gain by faking the Ferrier Dragon Rug.

Phillips prepared himself to wage war with the mysterious man who was said to speak the Queen's English. It would be a battle of wits, and he looked forward to the showdown.

Phillips had been born a skeptic and had trained as an archeologist. Little wonder, then, that he had made a name in his field by revealing archeological fakes. He loved to debunk. He lived to expose.

Phillips had made his reputation by impugning the honesty of a respected colleague forty years his senior, named Thad Jones, who had been famous for "discovering" an Anatolian-based, pre-historic cult of earth-goddess worshippers. Jones's discovery had been one of those lucky accidents. Traveling alone in the Anatolian countryside, he had stumbled on a hidden cave, and in it he had found a series of elaborate paintings on its walls. They depicted men bowing before powerful females with hands on hips. The female figures appeared to wear skirts, and Jones saw elements in them that suggested heavy breasts and fertile loins. Earth goddesses.

Unfortunately, Dr. Jones had run out of film and was unable to make a photographic recording of this phenomenal find. Luckily, though, he had brought along a sketchpad and colored pencils, and he did a remarkable job of illustrating what he saw. What he saw was amazingly like what can still be found in nearly any Turkish kilim: skirts, arms on hips, breasts, loins.

The trouble is that Jones was better at recording what he saw than where he saw it. He could never again find the cave, nor could any of his followers, mostly women, many of whom spent their vacations tromping all over the Turkish countryside looking for it.

Some years later, reviewing Dr. Jones's claims about earth goddesses, Phillips was skeptical, and he said so in a prestigious academic journal. For he had discovered that the same terrible luck had befallen Jones on a previous occasion, thirty years before his earth-goddess find. He had made another amazing discovery, which eventually became the topic of his Ph.D thesis, and this time, too, he had been without witnesses and had found himself without a camera and had had to sketch what he had discovered the best he could. Phillips had pointed out that that no doubt explained why Jones had thereafter been careful to carry along a sketchpad, but it hardly explained why he had not learned to be a little more careful about carrying photographic equipment. Anyway, Jones had lost the site of that find, too. So in both cases he was the only witness to his discoveries. Moreover, Phillips demonstrated pretty convincingly that the figure of the hands-on-hip earth goddess found in Jones's drawings and in Turkish kilims resembled the Anatolian dung beetle at least as much as it did a goddess. In short, Phillips really fried Jones, who soon retired. Phillips's reputation as a debunker was made.

Hence it was he whom Ulysses Pope engaged to judge the age and authenticity of an Oriental rug that seemed about ready to surface.

Well, he now knew the small man's name, and it wasn't Jake, as Holden what's-his-name had suggested. (In fact that young rug dealer had been no help at all, plus he wouldn't budge on the price of his Kazak. "A darned fine rug," Phillips thought. "Well, I'll grind him a little harder.") Other dealers had been much more useful. They all knew exactly whom he was talking about when he inquired about the small man who spoke the Queen's English. Avery Deane. Deane had snooped around every rug store in Berkeley and San Francisco, and everyone knew him. Or, rather, they knew his name but nothing else about him. Only that he frequented their shops, knew his stuff about old rugs, and that he had been at the talk that Ulysses Pope had given about himself.

"He was at a talk of Pope's?"

"Yes, he was in the audience. In fact, I hear that he joined the Ali Babas just like the rest of us. And then he dropped out like we all did."

"You joined and then dropped out?"

"We all did. Except for Sarah Atwood. She didn't drop out, but that's because she's trying to butter up the old codger so the Museum will get the Pope collection."

"But, anyway, where is this fellow Deane from? England?"

"Could be. That or maybe anywhere in the British Empire, if you know what I mean. I've never heard him say. But he sounds like the BBC. Or the Queen Mum. Crazy son of a bitch, though."

"What do you mean?"

They all had stories about his shouting and carrying-on. But no one knew much about him. Phillips decided to frequent rug stores in the hope of running into him.

Which is what happened. He walked into Holden Carter's showroom one day and was startled to hear angry shouting. His first impulse was to duck out quickly before a fight broke out. "Holden," a man inside the showroom yelled, "it's a fake! A fraud! It's nothing but a copy!" Phillips had found his man; he was certain of it. He was hearing the biggest voice *ever*, the voice of a circus ring-master, a general calling his troops to battle, a champion auctioneer. He was looking at a small, good-looking man with a sour expression on his face, standing beside the store's proprietor and frowning down on an Oriental rug spread on the floor between them.

"It's a good looking rug, Avery. I don't understand why you're so harsh about it," Holden argued.

"It is exactly what it appears to be: a new rug that somebody distressed to make it look old. But, of course, it doesn't look old at all. It looks like a new rug that is *supposed* to look old. *That's* why I'm hard on the rug. There is no mystery in it. There is no artifice, no art, no real deception."

Phillips wandered over to where the two were arguing and stared down at the victim of all this abuse, a new Turkish version of an old Bijar. They looked up at him and made way for the newcomer. The rug was quite attractive, Phillips thought. He was surprised that a new rug could look so good. "Does any of that matter?" he asked. "I mean, it's either a good rug or it isn't, right? If it looks good and it's made from good materials, why then it *is* good, isn't it? Does it matter if it's a reproduction?"

Deane laughed. "Strange that *you* should take that position—you, an archeologist, a lover of antiquities."

Phillips was flattered. The fellow recognized him. Still, he said to Deane, "Strange that *you* should take a stand against fakes."

At that, Deane laughed boisterously. Phillips imagined that he too was pleased to have been recognized, even if that meant being recognized as a forger of rugs. "Oh, I respect anything that is well done," Deane said brightly. "It's not what you do, it's how you do it. But this rug," (he pointed at the piece that lay on the floor at their feet, "is neither as good as the rug it's a copy of nor is it an honest new rug. Distressed to death! It's a brand new VW with 130,000 miles on it."

"But what if it *were* as good as what it is a copy of? Like those two Caucasian rugs in the Carpet Museum?"

"Oh, them." Deane was dismissive. "One can do better."

"That's frightening."

Deane laughed. "Not at all," he said. "It means that the art of making great rugs is still alive."

"And in the hands of criminals."

"Well. That depends on how good it is, doesn't it? If it's a work of art then it wasn't made by a criminal; it was made by an artist." Deane *looked* like an artist, Phillips thought, with his silk scarf and tweed beret and a cracked look on his face— a look at once of delight and annoyance.

"Made for criminal intent."

"To make money? Even artists need to live."

"Made with the intent to defraud."

"Ah, but intent is a complex matter, isn't it? I mean, even someone intending to defraud may have other intentions as well. To please, for instance. Or to make the best whatever-it-is the world has ever seen. Or to express himself."

"And the two Caucasian rugs in the Carpet Museum?"

"Oh, I would have to say they were done by a learner. So you could say they are mere copies. But then, perhaps their maker not only intended to deceive but also intended to learn, to practice, to perfect. At least they're good, unlike *this* mess." Deane pointed at the Turkish "Bijar." "Now *there's* a criminal, whoever made this sad thing." Phillips still thought it looked good.

"You're just playing with words," he said. "Fraud is fraud; deception is deception." He walked over to where the Kazak which he still hoped to buy at a good price from Holden what's-his-name was mounted on a wall. "Now this is a work of art, and I don't believe that its weaver deceived anybody, nor did she try to. The rug is what it is. It doesn't pose as something it is not. For instance, it does not pass itself off as a hundred years older than it really is."

"You're right! It is what it is. It's a Bentley. A Rolls! But it's not a work of art. It is a work of craft, just like a Bentley. Our honest weaver crafted it beautifully. But art it is not. And do you know why? Because it does *not* deceive."

"Oh *please*!"

Deane laughed his demented laugh. "Art is deception. Didn't you know that? The better the deception, the better the art. The swelling sounds of violins and cellos makes us feel like something sad has happened, and a sounding trumpet can make a weak man believe he's a hero. A poet can make us believe we are hearing the truth, when in fact we are hearing no more than his opinion. Now that's art."

Phillips smiled. He rather liked this strange fellow who at least had ideas. "Well, I see that I'm not going to change your mind, but, still, I find it worthwhile to distinguish between the genuine and the fake, between the hundred-year-old rug and the one that *seems* to be a hundred years old but is new."

Avery Deane was no longer smiling. "Congratulations," he said dryly. "You will spend your life searching out objects that are transparent fakes and that have no merit. Now *there's* a wasted life. While some seek out beauty and others *create* beauty, you make your livelihood and your name in the world by pursuing the ugly. You will be happy only if it is said about you that 'he has an unerring nose for the false, the ugly.' And on your deathbed you will gloat that you have surrounded yourself with more would-be art than anyone who has ever lived."

Marley Phillips had stopped smiling, too. He felt as if this wild spirit had just cursed him. Not sworn at him, but cursed him—as if Deane had commended his soul to hell. Though Phillips believed in neither the soul nor in damnation, still he felt a deep chill as the little man turned away from him and scuttled away like a crab.

Chapter Twenty-Five

There was a glow about it, an aura of *age*,
of wool polished and browned by centuries of use.

 When she took Deane's phone call at the Museum, Sarah was at her desk and had been thinking about him. She had spoken to him no more than three times and had seen him only twice: once when he had visited her at the museum and once at Pope's rally for the Ali Babbas. She recalled his stunning voice, the flair of his silk scarf, his chiseled though deeply lined face. It was almost a pity that she would have to sacrifice him if he actually brought her the Ferrier Dragon Rug. Because, given the fact that Avery Deane wanted cash and Pope wished to remain anonymous, the likely scenario was that Deane would hand over the rug to Sarah, she would pass it on to Pope, Pope would give her the money ($1,000,000 cash) for Deane, and she would keep the money—all of it. Of course Deane would raise bloody hell, but it would be her word (the curator of an important museum collection) against his (a person of obscure origins).

Oh, and she would also like to wind up with the $100,000 commission, for a total of $1,100,000. Pope would get his rug; she would get her money. Avery Deane would get nothing. Oh well.

While she was daydreaming about piles of green cash, the phone in her office rang and Deane, on the other end of the line, said, "I have something to show you, my dear." Sarah, who all her life had had nerves of steel, had to sit down.

"What is it you would like to show me?" Her voice quavered.

"A dragon, my dear. I think you're going to like him, have no fear." He laughed like a mad man, and she found herself laughing, too.

Finally she said, "Don't bring it here. Can you come to my home tonight?"

He laughed again.

When Sarah moved to San Francisco to take the museum job, she sold her brownstone in Washington. Instead of buying a house in San Francisco, she invested her considerable equity in liquid assets. Sarah lived in a flat in Sausalito that she leased by the year. She felt sure that she would not be in San Francisco forever and she wanted to be able to put her hands on her money quickly if she needed to.

Deane arrived downstairs at her security door, and through the video monitor mounted near the door, she could see that his neck was wrapped in a silk scarf, his head topped by a tweed beret, and one shoulder was draped with a rolled rug. When she walked downstairs and opened the door for him, she saw a taxi drive away behind him. Sarah shook his hand and led the way up the stairs to her door, which she opened for him. She did not and would not glance at the rug.

She was the gracious hostess. "Mr. Deane, it's so good of you to come. I know it's late. Can I pour you a glass of wine? Red? A Pinot Noir from the Russian River Valley?" He smiled while she pulled a cork and he flew about her living room like a humming bird, commenting on her *objets d'art*.

"A fine netsuke, my dear. Someone let it go. Imagine. Gave it up. Sold it! Hah, hah! You got it. That's what matters. But how *could* they, you know? Makes you wonder. Money troubles, probably. No sin in that." He was shouting, though she was just a few feet away. "But please," he said, "don't call me Mr. Deane. We're birds of a feather! How about Avery? Or Jack. Or Jake. Take your pick. Besides, I'd like to call you Sarah."

"I'd be pleased if you did," she said as she handed him a glass of wine. "But my goodness, how can I decide what to call you? I've never known anyone with so many names. I like Avery, though, and if you don't mind, that's what I'll call you."

"Why, Avery is fine. I chose it myself. So, Avery it is then. And Sarah." They clinked glasses.

"Shall I take your scarf and hat?" She said nothing about the object draped over his shoulder that she simply could not bear to acknowledge. He gave up his scarf and hat, revealing a shock of wavy brown hair that was beginning to gray over his ears. He sat in a chair to which she pointed, first shrugging the rug off his shoulder and dropping it to the carpeted floor beside him. Sarah had had many occasions to apologize to guests—many of them from the world of Oriental rugs—for her wall-to-wall carpeting, telling people that her landlord refused to let her pull it up to make way for hand made carpets, but the truth is that she preferred carpeting to Oriental rugs. In fact she had sold her Serapi along with her brick house in Washington, glad for the money and happy not to have the responsibility of maintaining it. The carpeting on which Deane had tossed his rug was plush and white. She loved it.

They made small-talk and sipped wine. Sarah thought Deane was a handsome man, but his face was disturbingly wrinkled in a pattern that suggested he was often annoyed. Yet now he was excited and enthusiastic. She found herself listening to his marvelous voice rather than to what he was saying. She was grateful that he did not once mention Oriental rugs, a subject in which she was, by circumstance, constantly having to pretend an interest. Instead he talked about his fascination with American "muscle cars" and the East Bay's park system, especially Tilden Park "with its creeks and eucalypts."

"They make me feel at home, the eucalyptus trees. Tilden Park must have the biggest concentration of them outside of Australia. They will burn, though! Grow fast, burn fast."

"So you're from Australia?"

"Oh yes, now and then. But I get bored and soon I'm from Botswana or London or New York. It really doesn't matter." She wasn't listening carefully except to the way he said eucalyptus and Botswana. Even "grow fast, burn fast." Everything he said sounded exotic or dangerous. "Muscle car."

"Another glass of wine?" she asked. She drained the bottle of Pinot Noir into their two glasses. He spoke of the Burgundian hillsides on which the grape was farmed. Finally there came a time when neither had spoken for a few moments, and both seemed to become aware at the same time that they had been staring at the back of the rolled rug lying on the white wall-to-wall. Sarah was embarrassed, as if she had been caught.

Deane had finally stopped smiling. "Well, my dear," he said, "I think it's time for you to meet our dragon." Still he stared at the rug's back, humming now.

"Avery, you know that I'll still have to show it to the collector? And I understand that he will have an expert on hand to authenticate it."

Deane finally looked away from the rug and at her. "Marley Phillips?"

"He didn't say, but that would be my guess." Deane's smile returned.

"Good! Wonderful! What fun!" He jumped up. Really *jumped* up and swooped the rug off the floor. He sprang with it to an open space in the room and faced Sarah, beaming. "Are you ready, Sarah?"

She felt weak, and, instead of standing up, she stayed seated and nodded to him. A million dollars was riding on this rug. Was it the Ferrier rug? Was it real? With a flourish as ancient as the rug trade itself, Deane held two corners of the rug and unfurled it in the air so that the other end landed on the floor. The rug, open now, faced Sarah, one end in Deane's hands and the other resting on the white carpeting, and at that angle it caught the light from a lamp. Slowly he pulled the rug straight and lowered his end until it lay before her like an offering.

First she saw color, a yellow gone amber with age. She rose and went to the rug and stood over it. There was a glow about it, an aura of *age*, of wool polished and browned by centuries of use. A dragon bristled on its amber background, a mad stare in its eyes. She knelt and ran the fingers of one hand across the rug, feeling it silky wool.

Deane walked around the rug and stood beside her and stared at it, too. He had quit his flourishing moves and had even stopped talking, and it was clear to her that he was deeply moved by the rug. He too dropped to his knees and felt the rug's age-softened wool. Suddenly she thought she understood: "He is not pretending. He believes in this rug. This is the real thing, the Ferrier Dragon Rug. Unless it isn't. Unless it's a fake. And it really doesn't matter, does it? The rug is that good." She had just met the first and only Oriental rug that she truly loved—or even liked.

Chapter Twenty-Six

"I'd rather have the rug, hang it on my wall and drink claret. We could sit there together and clink glasses."

 Deane might whistle in the graveyard: "I know you're going to love it Sarah dear ..." But who could tell what she might think? Until now, he had shown the finished version of the dragon rug to no one. Would she laugh at it? Was its purported antiquity transparently fake? Its dragon laughingly kitch? Despite his bravado, he could scarcely breathe as he laid his rug out before her.

When, instead of laughing, she ran her fingers over the rug's silky pile with a kind of reverence, he lost all doubt. Through her eyes he saw its glowing, age-browned colors, it's balance and harmony and its air of mystery. Of one thing he was now certain: With his magic he had created a mirage, a grand illusion, a heart-stopping deception. From earthworms and wool, roots and muck, and by his own artifice he had conjured a work of art. He wanted to spread it before Pope and Phillips and look them in the eye and dare them to call it a fake.

"But the collector wishes to be anonymous," Sarah argued. "He asked me to bring the rug to him myself. Then, if he approves, I'm to bring you the money."

"Hardly anonymous, Sarah. It's Ulysses Pope! Who else? Could anyone else pay a million dollars for a rug?"

"Still, I have to respect his right to privacy."

"Talk to him. Tell him I'm balking. And I am, you know. I'm tempted to keep it. I don't care about the money. I'd rather have the rug; hang it on my wall and drink claret. We could sit there together and clink glasses, you and I." Deane had settled into a sofa and she into a comfortable chair in Sarah's living room and while they talked they gazed at the dragon rug before them, spread on the white wall-to-wall. Now he turned in his chair and looked at her. "Let's keep it," he proposed, earnestly.

She wasn't sure just *what* he was proposing, but Sarah's eyes, though fixed on the rug, were steadfastly on the prize: a million dollars. Plus commission. "Avery, a deal is a deal. You knew the rules before you brought the rug by tonight. The collector remains anonymous. If you wanted to keep it, you shouldn't have come."

Deane was delighted by her spirit. "All right, my dear, let's sell it."

"Half for you and half for me?" she wondered, silently. She turned and looked at him and was certain that was exactly what he meant. "A half-million-dollars each and a life together," she said to herself, trying it out. She was interested in this unusual man. It's just that she had been thinking along the lines of a million dollars, free and clear.

Then he added, "But I still want to show it to Pope myself. And Phillips. I want to watch the famous debunker examine it."

Whatever else was going on, Sarah heard loudly and clearly that the scenario he was insisting on took the money

196

out of her hands. "If he delivers the rug to Pope, then Pope will pay *him* for it if he decides to buy it," she reasoned to herself. "No chance to put the money in my pocket. On the other hand, I could cast my lot with him and have half of the million dollars. I could keep working at the Museum and wait for other opportunities." All in all, it seemed to her as if a million dollars was startlingly more than $500,000. She decided not to settle for half of it and to keep looking for a way to keep it all.

"Okay, I'll phone," she said. Deane listened while she explained to Pope that the man with the Dragon rug wanted to deliver the rug to him in person. She added, on her own, that he wanted the money in cash upon delivery, not the next day or next week.

"Tell him 'no deal,'" Pope said. "Wait! You've seen the rug, right? How does it look?"

"It's the best rug I've ever seen, but of course I don't know whether it's the Ferrier rug. If I had to guess, I'd say it is."

"The best rug you've ever seen?"

"Yes. The best looking. Not the finest, but the most attractive."

"I don't give a damned whether it's attractive or not as long as it is the Ferrier rug!" Sarah could picture his scowl. "Why does he want to give it to me in person? Does he want to know who I am?"

"He assumes the buyer is Ulysses Pope. He thinks no one else has the money to buy this rug. My guess is that he wants to see your face when he shows you the rug. I think it's personal with him. He was hoping Marley Phillips would be there, too."

"Why?"

"Same reason, I think."

"I don't like this." A pause. "Okay, let's all meet the day after tomorrow. You and Deane be at the San Francisco Airport Hilton at 2:00 PM with the rug. I'll have the money in cash and I'll have Phillips there to inspect the rug. But before I pay, this man will have to sign a statement promising never to disclose any information at all about the rug: who the buyer is, where he got the rug, *that* he got it, how much I paid for it, *anything*. You'll have to do the same thing. It looks good, you say?"

"The rug?"

He grunted.

She turned and looked at Deane. "It looks fabulous. I just hope it winds up where it should: in a museum."

"Screw museums," Pope said. She silently agreed.

Off the phone now, Sarah left her chair with her glass of wine, kicked off her shoes and walked to the sofa, where she sat at the end opposite his. She turned in the sofa until she faced him, leaned back against the arm of the sofa and put her bare feet in his lap. "Avery, it is real, isn't it?"

"This little piggy," he said, wiggling one of her big toes. He smiled.

"But tell me the truth."

"Of course it's real. Does it matter?" He ran his hands over her calves, dabbing at the muscles and then smoothing them like a sculptor working a piece of clay.

"No, it doesn't matter. The rug is so good that it really doesn't matter whether it's the Ferrier piece or not."

"It gives me great pleasure to hear that you like it, my dear. I always thought you would, though I suspect you aren't a great fan of many other Oriental rugs."

She looked steadily at him for a moment, took a sip from her wineglass and said, "A very good guess. And a very big secret of mine. Are you shocked?"

He traced the long curves of her calves with his hands. "No," he said, "I'm not shocked. Most Oriental rugs are boring."

"Yes, and we still have to make a living, don't we? Take you. If you were to fake an Oriental rug for $1,000,000., who could blame you?"

"But that isn't it, Sarah. I told you before that it's not the money."

"Well, it is for me."

Deane laughed. "I don't know why I'm amused. I'm usually quite impatient with people whose focus is money. The stuff doesn't move me."

"Then give it to me," she said.

Deane laughed again, playfully slapped the bottom of one bare foot and scooted toward her so that now her knees were arched over his lap. "I don't have it yet, my dear—the million dollars cash."

"Let me take the rug to them. If you go, you'll just say something outrageous and blow the sale. When I sell it for you, you pay me a hundred-thousand-dollar commission."

He smiled and shook his head. "If I give you the rug I might not see it or you again, or the money. Besides, I want to be there to see what old Ulysses says, and I'd like to hear how Phillips advises him. That's what interests me." But he was interested in her knees, too, and he resumed his sculpting.

Chapter Twenty-Seven

"It's glorious, gentlemen, absolutely glorious! Fruit of the loom. Baked apples in brown sugar! Hah! You tell *me*!" In his stentorian voice and rounded vowels, you had to believe that he was shouting about something important.

 Two days later, Sarah and Deane asked a counterman at the airport Hilton to ring Mr. Pope's room, and in a moment Pope opened the door. Inside, Deane caught a dreary hotel-room smell and grimaced at the blue carpeting, white, bumpy bedspreads stretched as tight as skin on two double beds, and the closed drapes covering the street-side wall of the room. He thought that he much preferred sleeping in his Porsche than in rooms like this—though, unfortunately, right at the moment he didn't own a Porsche. Well, they came and they went. He would have another one soon. Deane wore the dragon rug on his shoulder, casually, just as he had at Sarah's. In addition, he wore his usual silk scarf and tweed beret and at one and the same time looked both fashionable and crumpled, like an English noble fallen on hard times. Inside, he shook hands with old Ulysses Pope and Marley Phillips, who towered over him, unpleasantly tall. Pope glowered and Phillips smiled, self-assured.

Deane instantly began pacing the room, saying whatever came to his mind: He laughed uproariously. "It's glorious, gentlemen, absolutely glorious! And you, too, missy. Fruit of the loom, I say. Baked apples in brown sugar! Hah! You tell *me*!" In his stentorian voice and rounded vowels, it was hard not to believe that he was shouting about something important. Still, it was nerve-wracking for the others to catch no sense of his meaning and to watch him heave about the room, especially so since he had the million-dollar-rug on his shoulder and, like a loose cannon, no one could tell what he might do next. When he suddenly strode toward the door, they closed on him to stop him from disappearing with the rug, but when he wheeled about and started back, they retreated as if he were dangerous.

This may have gone on for some time, but Pope growled, "Damn it, man, stay still. We didn't come here to watch you parade."

Avery Deane stopped close to Pope; in fact he stood much too close; was in his face, even. "You came to see a rug?"

"Well, Deane, what did you bring us?" Phillips beamed. He seemed ready for a good contest, like a well-prepped boxer dancing and bobbing before a bout. Or like a famous debunker, ready to score another win.

Sarah added her own challenge. "Yes, Avery, it's time to put up." Deane noticed that she called him by his first name. One of his first names.

"Or shut up? Hah, hah! Fat chance. But everybody watch-up now. Here's what you came for." With that, he made the same moves he had practiced so recently on Sarah: He pulled the rug off his shoulder and flung it into the air, keeping one end of it in his hands and letting it open toward the gawkers: Pope, Phillips and Sarah. He held it vertically it for a moment, letting its bottom end just touch the floor, and then he allowed the whole rug to settle atop the ugly blue carpeting. Ugly carpeting, smelly hotel room, hostile Pope, gorgeous, treacherous Sarah, combative Phillips, hypnotic dragon carpet. Its charge was not due to bright colors or anything lurid, but to its simplicity, its obvious antiquity and its time-softened colors. They all stared at the rug in undisguised wonderment. Here in one room, Deane noted, were Ulysses Pope, possessor of the world's most revered collection of Oriental rugs; Sarah Atwood, curator of a major museum's rug and carpet department and Marley Phillips, a scientist and rug-lover and famous debunker. They were staring open-mouthed at a rug that had sprung, as it were, from his loins.

No one said a word. No one moved. Finally, Phillips sat down on the floor, cross-legged, next to the rug and ran his hand over its surface. Then, in the age-old manner of rug experts, he flipped a corner and looked at its back. He looked at the rug front and back, back and front, focusing on ever-smaller details of its construction and materials, until finally, after carefully examining its knots, its selvage, the number of wefts between each row of knots and much else, he held the rug up to his nose and sniffed it. Then he flattened it out again on the blue carpeting and stood back and gazed at it a long while.

Deane's breathing grew troubled. Sarah's hands began to tremble and Pope's glare deepened to a glower. His foot began to beat on the blue carpeting.

"God damn it Phillips, speak up!" Pope thundered. "Earn your god damned money!"

Marley finally looked away from the rug. "Uh...." He started.

"But before you say anything," Pope interrupted, "it's a goddamned good rug. Anyone can see that. It looks real to me. You're always knocking things down. Think about it."

Phillips studied Pope a moment longer and then turned his attention back to the rug. "It's just that his left eye is strange, isn't it? The dragon's left eye? I mean, the rest of the rug seems right. It's old. It's as old as dirt. The dyes are good. Its construction is right. But why didn't Ferrier mention that its left eye is half closed? Look at that."

They all peered at the dragon's eyes. Its left eye did seem...different. Sarah Atwood looked up and took in young Marley Phillips's look of puzzlement and then glanced at old Ulysses Pope's fierce scowl and then finally at Avery Deane. For the first time today, his wrinkled face was smiling.

"Of course I haven't yet tested it with the spectrometer." Marley added. "That's the next step."

Sarah spoke up. "But Mr. Deane stipulated that you'll have to decide right now whether you want it and then pay for it if you do."

Deane needed to move around. Soon he was pacing through the hotel room as wildly as before, nearly running, but then he stopped and faced Pope and Phillips. He stared first at Phillips and demanded, "But what do you *think*, man? You're the expert on fakes. Is it real or not?" Then he glared at Pope. "Ulysses Pope, I want to know what you think. You're the world's preeminent rug collector. Do you like it or don't you? Is it worth a million dollars or not? Or shall I keep it and enjoy it on my wall?"

"Oh, for God's sake," Pope growled, "calm yourself! Of course I like it. It's marvelous." It sounded as if he meant it. "But first Phillips is going to have to give me word that it's the real thing, and, if he does, I'm still going to require that you promise in writing to disclose nothing at all about the rug, like where you got it, who you sold it to or for how much."

"But you like it?"

"If I buy it, it will be the best rug in my collection."

With that, Deane did calm down. In fact suddenly he looked serene, and he turned to Phillips and asked, conversationally, "Is it real?"

"The rug is wonderful," he answered. "But is it Chinese? All the technical things are right: its foundation material, its knot, it's selvage, spin, ply, colors. But anybody could have done that at any time, including you. And if it is Chinese, is it the Ferrier rug? The design is right. It's what Ferrier described except for that eye. The dragon has the correct number of toes, for instance. But, again, anyone could have designed it at any time, including you.

"The real question," Phillips went on, "is whether it's old enough, because if it is, it almost doesn't matter whether it is the rug Ferrier reported on. Right? Because it *could* be. And because it's splendid."

"Well, *is* it old enough?" Deane pressed.

"It looks like it is. It smells like it is. By the way, I'd say it was exposed to dampness at some time in its existence. There is the slightest suggestion of mildew in the way it smells.

"There are only two ways we might be able to tell whether it is old enough. The first is to analyze its dyes. If any of them prove to be synthetics, then we're certain that it is no more than about 135 years old, which is when the first of the synthetic were invented. If all the dyes are natural, then the rug may be genuinely old—but not necessarily so. The other method is to subject the rug's materials to a number of tests in the lab. There's a problem with that, though. We could probably get no closer than about 150 years to the rug's actual age. Anyway, you asked me if the rug is old enough to be the Ferrier Dragon Rug, and I have to say my guess is yes. Frankly, it's one thing to make a new rug look a hundred years old—again, something you could do—but quite another matter to make it look nearly 400 years old. With all respect, Mr. Deane, I don't believe that even you can do that."

Avery Deane had lost interest. Pope liked the rug and Phillips believed it was real. Good. His mind strayed. He daydreamed about stretching out on the fully-reclined seat of a Porsche 928, parked under an oak tree and gazing through a moon-roof at the stars. He wondered whether Sarah might like that as well. He thought about where he might like to go next. Stay here in the States for a while longer? Back to London? Or maybe even go home? As he signed Pope's pledge not to reveal anything about the rug, he thought briefly about the cash that had suddenly appeared in a large briefcase on one of the double beds. But as Pope counted it out for him in hundred-dollar bills, Deane's mind turned back to other things. "Buy a white one this time. See if I can find one with a moon roof. A moon roof! That's it! Gaze at the stars all night!"

Deane had left with the briefcase that contained a million dollars. Sarah, Pope, and Phillips still stood gazing at the dragon rug. Sarah stayed behind to collect her ten percent commission and also because she hated to think she may not again ever see the rug. Even worse, she might never again possess it as, to some degree, she had for two or three days. During that time, anything had been possible. She might have put it in a suitcase and taken it to Rio. She might have shared a million dollars and her life with Avery Deane. There had been the outside chance that she could manage to possess both the rug *and* a million dollars cash—though that would surely have meant having to hide forever from the rich and no-doubt vengeful Ulysses Pope.

Well, the rug was out of her control now—unless Pope donated it to the Museum. "He might," she thought. "What can I do to make sure he does?" That's what she thought about as she stood before the rug, Pope beside her. Soon they all broke off looking at the rug, and the wealthy old industrialist wrote her a check for $100,000. Before she left she threw her arms around him and kissed his cheek. Phillips, surprised, looked away. Pope's face turned ruddy and he held her a moment and gazed into her face. Finally he growled and let her go.

"I know one thing," Sarah said to herself as she made her way out of the hotel. "If I ever get my hands on a million-dollar rug again, I'm never going to let go of it." And as she settled into the back seat of a taxi, she asked herself, "Is it real? Was that the Ferrier Dragon Rug?" By the time the cab was on the freeway and heading for San Francisco, she had reached a conclusion. "It is now."

Still in the hotel room, Pope and Phillips were silent for some time after Sarah left. Phillips needed to know why Pope had practically forced him to authenticate the rug. After all, Pope knew full well that the only way the rug could be decisively certified was to test it in the lab, and yet Pope had agreed to the absurd condition that payment for the rug could not wait a week for testing. Why?

Pope broke the silence. "There's no point in testing the rug for its age, is there?" It didn't sound to Phillips like a question. "In the lab, I mean. Carbon dating and all that."

"Do you want me to?" Phillips asked.

"Of course not."

He had to think about that. Why didn't Pope want him to determine the rug's age? Well, that wasn't so hard to figure out. Pope had just paid a million dollars for it. What if it turned out to be a fake?

"What can you do," Pope asked, "to make testing impossible if some hotshot debunker like you used to be decides to carbon date it? Is there anything you can do to screw up the results of future testing?"

"No. There is no way to make testing ineffective or misleading."

"But, of course, if you tested it yourself and found that it was old enough, then no one else would have to test it."

"But you said you don't want me to."

"You don't have to. All you have to do is say you did. After that, why would anyone else bother to test it?"

Pope was asking him to fake the results of scientific testing. He was asking him to bless the rug with his respected professional name. He began to consider the reasons why he should do it. After all, the rug *might* be the Ferrier Dragon Rug. He really did not believe that Deane or anybody else could make a new rug look that old. He also believed that it would be quite nice to be known as the ultimate authority to whom Pope had turned to authenticate the rug. But he was still puzzled about one thing.

"But why?" he asked the old rug collector.

"Because I want to own the Ferrier Dragon Rug."

That made sense to Phillips. Who wouldn't want to own it. "Well, Ulysses, let's talk about my professional fees, and if we can work that out, you *will* own the Ferrier Dragon Rug."

Alone, with two hours to kill before returning to the airport and then back home with the rug scrunched into his carry-on luggage, Pope gloated. "I bought the Ferrier Dragon Rug," he thought, "for the measley price of a vacation home in the country: $1,100,000." He chuckled. He, alone, was not confused. Deane, Sarah and Phillips may not quite get it, and maybe no one ever would. But he did: "That man, Deane," he thought, "is a genius. I just got an original Deane for barely over a million dollars And it's the best work he's ever done."

Chapter Twenty-Eight

"Better get mobile," he concluded.
"That's the first thing. New wheels."

 Forty minutes after he left San Francisco Airport in the backseat of a taxi, and now parked in front of Sandra Smith's apartment building in Berkeley, Deane pulled a hundred-dollar bill from his briefcase, gave it to the Indian driver and told him to keep the considerable change. The fellow eyed Deane's briefcase and for a moment he hesitated, as if company policy prohibited him from accepting large bills pulled from a briefcase, but he reconsidered and the hundred-spot quickly vanished. Deane started for the building, then remembered the briefcase which he had left in the backseat of the cab. Luckily, the driver was twisted in his seat, still eyeing the briefcase on the back seat. He hadn't yet pulled away, and Avery was able to retrieve his property.

He walked past Sandra Smith's door, wondering whether she was at home. He was startled suddenly to remember that he owed her for three month's unpaid rent. "Funny," he thought, "I haven't thought about paying rent in a long time and she hasn't said a word. Well, I'll see her later." Honestly, he hadn't thought about Sandra at all for the past week or so, ever since he had finished the rug and had been preparing to show it to Sarah. Until then they had been spending quite a lot of time together. Of course he had been without a car for some time and she had taken him here and there—including to Oregon to find Cherise Hollander. "Hmm, I owe her, too: Cherise. Don't remember how much. Maybe I wrote it down." He had talked Cherise into advancing him all of the naturally-dyed wool that went into the dragon rug. "Well, that was a good investment for her," he thought, inaccurately. "And Khalil. Don't know how much I owe him. Quite a bit. Have to ask."

He climbed the stairs to his apartment, flipped on a light by the door and stood quietly, feeling the room's emptiness. While once it was filled with Zainab, Soroya, Katija, and Fatima plus Sandra and himself and later filled by the loom and Khalil and always a person or two watching the work progress line by line, now the room was nearly empty except for dark, Victorian-looking furniture and doilies spread on every surface. During the past several days the dragon rug— at times spread on the floor and at other times pinned to the wall like a painting, and sometimes draped over his bed—had seemed to fill the studio apartment, even though the rug was small and there had been none other than himself in the room to admire it. Now it was gone, and in its place was a briefcase full of money.

"Hmm. Guess I owe the spinners, too. And then there's Holden. He never got the silk Kerman, did he? Hate to give them money, though. Just doesn't seem right. They all deserve better." Deane thought for a while, still standing in his doorway, studying the emptiness of his room. "Better get mobile," he concluded. "That's the first thing. New wheels. Believe I'll go see Holden. He's always up for a lark." Deane still held his briefcase, so all he had to do was to turn off the light and back out of his door.

Holden was skeptical. He had stood by in the past while Deane had peaked the hopes of many a would-be seller, including Judge Barron in Napa who had hoped to sell him his Rolls Royce. Nothing ever came of these encounters except, ultimately, the disappointment of the sellers. Holden doubted that Deane had had any money as he had teased the hopeful would-be sellers, and he doubted that he had any money now as he put a salesman through his paces at the Oakland Porsche dealership. Deane had explained to Holden that Porsche quit making its eight-cylinder 928 model after 1989, so he was here to look at the new Porsche 911s, which started at around $70,000.

Deane had declined the young, snappy salesman's invitation to test-drive a new metallic-blue Porsche. Instead, after walking around the car a time or two and scowling at it, he asked to inspect the driver's-side seat adjustments. Ultimately, Austin, the Porsche salesman, failed Deane's request to make the seat fully recline. Austin protested that *no* car seat fully reclines, and, besides, why would anyone want a car seat to flatten out? Deane sneered at the fellow. "Oh, no car seat reclines?" he asked sarcastically. "Not even on the 928? But of course you're an ignorant pup and wouldn't know about a noble car that ceased to be made when you were in grammar school. Austin, I have shoes older than you are. Come on, Holden. Let's find a real automobile."

By that evening, Deane had bought a 1983 white Porsche 928 with 110,000 thousand miles on the odometer. He paid

$3,800 in cash for it and was extremely pleased. Holden was surprised that he actually had some money and he contemplated reminding Deane that the silk Kerman had still failed to materialize. But, as always, he considered how Deane had turned his business around, and he found himself unwilling to make an issue of it.

As Deane was buckling his seat belt to drive his new car home and Holden was heading toward his own car, he remembered that he had a message for Deane. He put his hands on the door of Deane's Porsche and asked through the open window, "Avery, do you remember the old farmer, Clem Briano?"

"Of course I do, Holden. The man with the tractor and the sixty acres of Cabernet."

"Yes. He called me, trying to get in touch with you. He said that he sold twenty acres of the property just like you suggested, but he says that now he needs to sell the rest, the forty-acre parcel with the ninety-year-old vines. He's no longer able to do the work himself and he wants to sell them to you. You made a good impression on him when you told him to keep the property. He'll make you a good deal."

Deane straightened in his bucket seat; he twisted and looked thoughtfully at Holden. "Hmm. Put down roots. Make wine. Quit the rug game." As he spoke, he patted a briefcase in the passenger seat beside him. "Well, lad, let's go see Clem tomorrow. But do you mind if we take my car? You can buy the gas."

So Holden was witness to Deane's next purchase, too. It was a deal put together by two men who would rather not involve realtors or attorneys. Clem slowly typed it out on an old Underwood and both men signed. Holden witnessed and signed as well. The terms were: $2,500,000 selling price; $980,000 down; the balance of $1,520,000, carried by the seller at 10%, was to be paid at $8,000 per month beginning as soon as the buyer could produce a profit from the property or within two years, whichever came first; sale to include all rolling stock, among which were a pickup truck and several tractors; sale to include fifty barrels of homemade cabernet sauvignon wine. And that was it. Deane counted out $980,000 in cash. He complimented Clem for his voice and his "dialect." They all went outside and the farmer showed Deane how to operate the tractor. They walked around and Clem pointed out this and that and offered some advice here and there. By the time Holden and Deane left, Clem was nearly in tears, not because of having just sold his beloved vineyard, but because he hated to see Deane leave.

Deane was exuberant as they drove back to the city. He sang. He raved about the vineyard, the view, the climate and Clem's honest attitude. His voice was stratospheric. Holden was in shock. Finally he asked, "Avery, where did you get that much cash?"

"I sold a rug, lad."

"A rug..."

"Don't ask. Not allowed to tell."

Holden felt plastered to his seat, he was so surprised by the whole, unlikely event. But he was worried. "I hope you held some money back, Avery."

"I did. I did."

"I mean for sales tax on the house and property tax, too. Right? Aren't you going to have to pay taxes?"

Deane frowned, but he wasn't going to be denied his celebration. "Oh that will all work out," he said with confidence. "It always does."

Of course, prudently, he *had* held back money: about $15,000. With it he paid Sandra, Khalil, the spinners and Cherise Hollander. At the same time, he put them all on the payroll again, all except Sandra. He commissioned them to make another rug. "I never got to see the last one after it was finished, boss." Khalil said.

"This one's going to be even better," Deane told him.

Of course, to say that he put Khalil and the others on the payroll was an exaggeration. Deane had grossly misjudged the amount of money he should have held onto. In order to record the purchase of the vineyard he would have to pay all kinds of fees and taxes—an absurd amount; an outrageous and even maddening amount, Deane felt, and for some time he was in a rage. Finally, though, he realized that, really, the matter was between him and Clem. If Clem knew he had sold the place and Deane knew he had bought it, and Holden had witnessed the exchange, then it was their own business and there was no reason to get the bureaucrats involved. That way, by not bothering to record the sale, he was able to avoid a great many expenses.

Still, he had to go to Holden and ask for a loan of $5,000. "Tide me over, sort of thing," he explained. "Forgot about petrol and all that driving back and forth to the farm." In fact, he hardly had time even to visit his new digs. It would have been splendid if he could have staged the new rug project in the Napa Valley—gorgeous country in which to bring a new rug into being—but neither the spinners nor Khalil would be able to commute that far. So Deane had to keep the studio apartment and hope that Sandra would be kind about the rent money. And he had to count on his production team not to need wages right away.

Holden had been a little prickly about the loan. "What happened to all that cash you had?" he asked.

"I spent it. You were there, man. Were you blind?"

"But…"

"I can't very well bring in the whole crop myself, now can I? Have to hire someone to harvest the grapes. That kind of thing costs money. Have to spend it to make it, right? And then we'll be rolling in money. Coming out of our ears! I'll pay you back in the Fall plus I'll throw in a barrel of Cabernet, one of Clem's."

"Have you forgotten about the Kirman? I still haven't seen it."

"Patience, lad. Worth waiting for."

Of course Holden had sprung for the $5,000 as Deane knew he would. "The boy has a good heart. All those others took advantage of him: that old pirate, Ulysses Pope. Had Holden out there driving him around, getting together a bunch of his customers for the Ali Babbas and then he wouldn't let him join. Well, we're going to get even, aren't we? Holden will hold that old man in the palm of his hand."

But what about Sarah? Deane had been right: She had loved the dragon rug. That wasn't the problem. The problem was that she had turned down a chance to keep it. "It could have been on her wall right this moment and I could have been pouring her a glass of Pinot Noir as we admired it. But she wanted the money. Can't blame her, even if it's not my thing. She probably wouldn't fancy sleeping in my car. Good enough for me, though. Under the stars." Then he remembered his vineyard and the farmhouse, tucked away in the rolling Tuscany hills of the Napa Valley. "It doesn't seem real, does it? Too good to be true. We'll have to get out there again and have a party or something. Have a go at that wine in the barrels. The whole gang. Holden and his girlfriend, Khalil, the spinners, Sandra. I think I'll forget Sarah. I'll bet Sandra wouldn't mind sleeping in a Porsche in a pinch. You can look right up at the stars through the moon roof. That's what I like."

Chapter Twenty-Nine

It was astonishing how loudly the small child could sing.
Her piping filled the chamber so that those closest to
her actually took a couple of steps backwards.

 Three months had passed since Deane bought
Clem's vineyard. He had been annoyed to find
that he had not succeeded in ducking certain
tax obligations. For instance, the County of
Napa had billed Clem Briano $38,000 for property taxes,
which was absurd, of course, because Clem was no longer the
owner. *He* was. But if they thought he had $38,000, they
were crazy. No one could get that much money together
when there had hardly been time to harvest any grapes at all
and now it would be next year before he could get any grapes
to market. Well, Napa County would just have to wait for its
tax money.

Anyway, these days, if he wanted to visit the farm he had
to get Holden or Sandra to pay for the petrol. And even then,
the utilities had been turned off in the house and it wasn't
much fun to be there without lights and heat and all the rest.

There was one bright spot, though. Two, actually: the wine
that Clem had sold with the house was superb! And there
were still 48 barrels of the stuff. Secondly, the new rug had
come along splendidly. Everyone had pitched in, excited
about the new project. The spinners had produced large

baskets of hand-spun wool in a very short time. It was wonderful to see them filling the little apartment with their industry and their singing. Cherise had done her magic, too, dyeing the yarn in record time. Khalil had taken another leave from his restaurant and had happily strung his loom for the new rug. This time, his hands flew from the very start and at the end of each day he could boast at least two inches of progress. The rug was off the loom in just two months, and now, already, Deane had dug it up from its muddy grave by the banks of Strawberry Creek in Tilden Park, where he had been careful to avoid park rangers. He had hosed it off and dried it and brushed it smooth, and he was admiring it as its glow filled his small apartment—when the phone rang.

"Avery, did you hear that they found the Ferrier Dragon Rug?" It was Holden. He was excited.

"I'm not surprised to hear it, lad."

"*I* am! What are the chances of that rug being discovered nearly four hundred years after Ferrier wrote about it, and in good condition? It's incredible! And here's the best part. Apparently Sarah Atwood from the Museum managed to land the rug for a one-night private preview next week by the Bay Area Rug Society. Want to go see it?"

"My car, your gas," he answered.

Of course, this was the rug-event of the decade, and everyone came: Sarah, as curator of the museum's carpet collection, hosted the event; Holden came and brought his girlfriend, Laura. Of course he invited Avery Deane who brought along Sandra; unknown to Avery Deane, Holden also invited Khalil, who brought Kammi and Star. Tom, who nearly a year earlier had bought Holden's Bijar and had come along to Little Kabul where they discovered Khalil, came, too. All of Holden's rug-dealer friends were there; the many collectors who for three years had showed Holden the rugs they had bought from his competitors and who finally, now, were buying rugs from him—they were there, too. And then, to crown the event, Ulysses Pope tottered in like royalty, accompanied by Marley Phillips, Kyle Berman from the Carpet Museum and Charles Evans Green, the grand old man of the Oriental rug world.

Holden, one of the most forgiving and charitable of all people, was not happy to see Pope. Pope had never thanked him for putting together the meeting in which he had solicited membership in the Ali Babbas (but had not accepted Holden's application), nor had he apologized, nor had he in any way made good for having taken scandalous advantage of Holden in a number of ways. Holden's face burned with embarrassment, thinking back on it. But it didn't matter. The old man was there, and he acted like he *owned* the Ferrier rug. Which was a thought. *Did* he own it? Pope's kingly air said yes. His patronizing pose said he was the rug's owner. And one could guess that Pope, of all people, was the one and the only person who had the money and clout to collect it.

But it didn't matter. The rug, occupying one wall of room by itself and lit by a host of spotlights that enhanced the warmth of it's colors—the rug was astonishing, gorgeous, simply beyond compare, a work of art of the first order. It was far more than an artifact. Holden was moved almost to tears by it.

All those in the room had drawn up before the rug and were silently taking it in. Deane and Sandra came in a little later than the others and moved to Holden's side. "Avery, have you ever seen anything so beautiful?" Holden whispered. Deane seemed pleased but not terribly interested. "Really, Avery, look at it!" Holden quietly insisted. But Deane was staring at Khalil, who was at the very front of the crowd, so close to the rug that he could have tasted it if he had stuck out his tongue. Khalil turned away and began jerking on Kammy's sleeve, pointing at the rug and excitedly whispering something to her. He pointed to his chest with a thumb and then at the rug with a finger; then to himself again. He was attracting attention. Sarah Atwood, Marley Phillips and Ulysses Pope were standing together just opposite Khalil on the other side of the rug and very near it. Though Holden couldn't hear what Khalil was saying, apparently the three rug Titans could, and they were obviously very unhappy. All three glared at him with obvious ill will.

Holden glanced at Deane, who was still at his side but who had become quite still and pale. Then Deane dashed away toward where Khalil and his family were standing. Before he could reach Khalil, though, something unexpected happened. Khalil's daughter, Star, looked around at all the people who were staring either at the rug or at her gesticulating father, and she believed that they were looking at her. Ever the performer, she believed that they were all here to hear her sing, and with that she took a stance directly before the dragon rug, faced her audience, threw open her arms in the age-old manner of people who belt out songs and launched into Somewhere Over the Rainbow. It was astonishing how loudly the small child could sing. Her clear piping filled the chamber so that those closest to her actually took a couple of steps backwards. Khalil reached out to stop her, but Kammy,

220

with a mother's fond smile, waved him off, evidently thinking that, once she was started, it was best to let Star finish her song. By this time, Deane had reached Khalil and he took him by his arm and hustled him away from the crowd.

Holden was confused. He watched as Khalil continued to point to the rug and then to himself, even as Deane got a kind of hammerlock on his other arm and more or less dragged him even further away from the others. As Star sang the lines about wishing on a star, which she sang with extra feeling, Deane was saying something in Khalil's ear and Sarah, Phillips and Pope were glaring in turn at Khalil, Deane, and at Star. Finally Star's song ended, she curtsied, the crowd clapped uncertainly, and she returned to her mother's side. Khalil returned to them but kept a little distance now between the rug and himself and, though he still seemed upset, he no longer spoke or gestured.

When Deane came back to where Holden, Laura and Sandra still stood, he glowered at Holden. "So, it was you who invited him to come?" he growled.

"Well, why not?" Holden asked innocently. "What's going on?"

"Khalil was up there telling everyone he made that rug."

Holden laughed. "When, four hundred years ago?" By this time, Sarah stood facing the audience where Star had stood moments before. She held a laser pointer and began lecturing, speaking first of the 17th century Ferrier account of a certain dragon rug. She read aloud Ferrier's description of the rug as it had been translated by Martin a hundred years ago, and then she pointed out the similarities between that description and the rug mounted on the wall before them. Holden was enthralled as the story unfolded.

"Therefore," Sarah announced, "the Museum has concluded that it is most likely that this, ladies and gentleman," and here her arm swept the air before the rug in a motion that was remarkably similar to Star's theatrics, "is the Ferrier Dragon Rug. Of course it will never be possible to be completely certain, but let's just say that we feel 99% certain that it is."

Throughout her talk, the crowd had often murmured and had even oooh-ed and ah-ed. "Do you have any questions?" she asked.

"Who owns the rug?" someone from the audience asked.

"The owner, who has graciously loaned it to us for a very short while, wishes to remain anonymous. But I'm sure you are as grateful to him—or her—as we are." Everyone looked at Ulysses Pope, who looked pleased with himself.

"Wait!" Khalil shouted. Sarah glared at him.

"Well, what?" she demanded.

He opened his mouth and then looked around the room as if looking for someone or remembering something. When he didn't speak, Sarah called for other questions.

Someone asked, "How can you be certain the rug is as old as the Ferrier rug would have to be?"

"I will let Dr. Phillips address that," she said, and she handed the pointer over to Phillips who was beside her. He proceeded to describe in detail a series of tests he had conducted on the rug to determine its age and concluded that it was between 300 and 500 years old.

"Please look for my article about all this in "Ancient Arts Magazine" in the fall," he added.

After that, Kyle Berman said a few very respectful words about the rug and finally Charles Evans Green, now quite old, said, "I don't know what this rug is. I suppose it's the Ferrier rug. Maybe not. Maybe it's brand new. But I've never seen a rug more beautiful in my life. I'm glad I've lived so long."

And that was it. That was the showing. Holden was so excited that he couldn't sleep that night, even though Laura rubbed his fevered brow.

Chapter Thirty

"Sprites are careless about money. They will say anything; do anything. It's all the same to them."

 During the year since Avery Deane had appeared in Holden's lonesome store, pacing and snarling and shouting at him to "Lock 'em up," Holden's life had changed for the better, even though he had not taken Deane's advice to lock up his rugs. Instead he had sold them. At first he had tried selling them the same way Deane did, by stomping around and shouting and comparing them to Mercedes Benz automobiles. Holden had tried standing a little too close to customers, had experimented with being overbearing, and had sometimes been obnoxious. It didn't suit him. He was embarrassed by his behavior. He would bully a customer and then excuse himself. He would cajole and then apologize. His customers were embarrassed, too. They left the store. During this time of experimentation, he didn't sell anything at all, though Deane continued to sell Holden's rugs right and left by using the same methods.

But there came a time when he discovered his own way of selling, and there was no trick to it at all: With Deane's support, Holden eventually became confident that his rugs were wonderful, and he stopped assuming that no one would ever buy them. Even though he now kept a respectful distance from his customers and did not take them by the elbow, and though he neither tricked nor bullied them, they began to buy from him.

From the very beginning, Deane had gossiped with him about the rug scene in London, Hamburg, Paris and Zurich. He had dropped names of famous rug people throughout the world, telling stories about them. All the while, he talked as if Holden were a fellow insider. Slowly, Holden began to believe that he actually was part of the rug world and not an imposter. And when he began to communicate his new confidence to customers—well, *that* sold rugs, too.

Of course, in the next breath after gossiping conspiratorially about a famous rug scholar, Deane would ask to borrow $1,000. Then later he would talk Holden into investing in a rug that never materialized. And then, finally, he would borrow another $5,000. So it was hard for Holden to feel unmitigated, joyous gratitude toward Deane. In fact, Holden became angrier and angrier as he felt more and more foolish for letting himself be taken advantage of.

He tried to explain it to Laura. "I have no idea of who he is. I don't know where he comes from. I don't know whether he is a real figure in the rug world...and I guess I don't care. It's just that I don't know. I don't know whether he's rich or poor. Is he a good guy or a bad guy? He won't take money from me when he sells one of my rugs. But on the other hand he won't pay me back what he owes me. He's bossy. He's exciting. He gets everyone engaged. He takes advantage of everyone. He's generous. He's grumpy. So who is he?"

"What do you think?" Laura asked.

Holden closed his eyes and thought. "I think I'm missing something I need to know about him before I'll understand who he is. I mean, someday I'll learn that he spent fifteen years in prison for embezzlement and everything will make sense. Or I'll find out that he is enormously wealthy and that will explain it all. Or whatever. Maybe he's a mad-man. I don't know what it will be, but something's missing."

About a week after the private viewing of the Ferrier Dragon Rug at the museum, Holden got the clue he needed. Deane showed up at the showroom, as grouchy as he had been the first time he had appeared. He didn't even glance at Holden but began stalking the store from one mounted rug to the next. He looked at the price tag of one and he threw his arms in the air in exasperation. "*Giving* them away!" he shouted. "Well, I've done the best I could. I wash my hands. The pup won't learn."

"Uh oh," Holden thought. "He's in a foul mood. What next?" Deane carried a rug over his shoulder. It was wrapped in white butcher paper, but it was obvious to Holden by the way it flopped that it was a rug.

"Here's your damned silk Kerman. Hope you're happy." Deane tossed the package onto the floor beside where Holden stood. "I'm moving on."

Wait. The silk Kirman? He had long ago decided that it was a fiction. Avery was moving on?

"You're what?"

"Going. Fleeing. Flying. Running. Jumping bail. Driving off into the sunset. It's time, lad." Deane's sonorous voice had softened. For the first time since he had burst into the store he looked at Holden.

"But Avery..." Holden didn't know what to ask first. "What about Sandra?"

He twirled away and resumed his dash from rug to rug. Staring for a moment at a recent discovery of Holden's, an old Bashir prayer rug, he answered, "What about, what about, what about! What about Sandra? She wants to know where I'm going. Hah! You tell me!"

"She won't come?"

"Doily unit! She won't be parted from it or the other rooms. The damned place is her life. I told her I have two reclining seats: driver's and passenger's. She wasn't impressed." He laughed, not bitterly, and he came back to where Holden was standing by himself.

"And the vineyard?"

"Do you want it? No title. No income. Damned vines just hanging on. They're ninety years old and if I stay I'll be the one who killed them. Tax bills come every day. It's a tragedy, though, about the wine. 45 barrels of fine Napa cabernet and I can't get even one of them in my hatchback."

Holden wondered vaguely about how he might manage to send them to Deane, wherever he was going. Actually, there really might be some way. A train or something. "Where will you go?"

"Hah!" Avery looked restless again. He tapped a toe of one shoe on the floor.

"But Avery, I was there. You have nearly a million dollars into that place."

Deane shrugged impatiently as if Holden had missed the point. "I have the car. Free and clear." He looked at Holden, not unkindly. "Listen, lad, take my advice. Throw that silk Kirman down your famous black hole of Calcutta. Leave it wrapped. Forget about it. Open it someday when you're old and famous and you'll remember me."

Holden felt confused. Avery had become more and more of a problem for him, causing scenes in his shop, demanding to be driven around, borrowing money, ranting and even raving, killing time in the rug store when Holden had work to do. Many times he had wished that Avery would disappear. But now, hearing that he was leaving, Holden suddenly felt almost frightened, as if he were being left behind. "Well, uh, thanks for the rug. I didn't think I'd ever see it."

"Should have trusted me. Right, lad?" Avery smiled a huge, ironic smile.

"I did," Holden protested. Actually, he hadn't. Still didn't.

Avery straightened his beret and pulled his scarf tighter around his neck. "Well, time to toddle off. Remember, lad: don't give 'em away. And publish, that's the thing. Publish or parish! Write a novel!" He stuck out his hand and Holden shook it and watched as Deane crossed the sidewalk in front of the store. Avery turned back and looked at Holden briefly and said, "Only one more thing to do before I flee. I have to return a book to the library." With that, he flung himself into his white Porsche and roared away from the curb.

Holden shook his head. Back inside his shop, he wondered what was in the package. It was about the right size to be a silk Kirman, he supposed. But why had Avery suggested that he not open it? It could be anything. It was also about the right size and weight to be a worn-out Hamadan. Holden carried the package across his showroom floor and then through the curtain to his apartment, then to his bedroom to which the black hole of Calcutta opened. But instead of throwing the package down its mouth, he pulled the tape from the paper and opened the package.

One by one Deane's victims showed up at the store, wondering whether Holden knew where he had gone. The four Afghan women were the first: Zainab, Soroya, Katija and Fatima. They hadn't been paid for the last work they did for him. Then Sandra. Deane owed her for rent, though it was obvious that her regrets had to do with losing him rather than anything having to do with money. Khalil came, Kammy and Star in tow. Khalil asked if he knew where the boss was. Clem Briano showed up, wondering what the hell had happened to Deane. He had had to reclaim his property and pay back taxes and save his vines from death. What the hell was he supposed to do about all the money Deane had paid for the place? Cherise Hollander phoned him from Oregon asking if he knew anything about Avery Deane. He had stiffed her for a bunch of dyeing-work she had done for him. Even Judge Barron called up Holden, wondering whether Deane might have changed his mind and might like to buy his Rolls Royce after all. Many people drifted in over the next several months looking for Deane. He owed them all money. A fellow came in who claimed that Deane owed him either money or a silk Kirman, whichever. An investigator from the Claremont Hotel said that Deane had freeloaded there many times during the past year, eating at the expense of various trade-groups. Holden assured all of them that he had no idea where Deane had gone and that he doubted Deane even had a plan.

One day Marley Phillips visited his shop, wondering whether he knew where Deane had gone. Phillips was not surprised to learn that no one knew of Deane's whereabouts. During his visit, he called Deane a genius but did not explain his thinking. And he bought a rug from Holden, paying full price.

And, finally, Sarah Atwood phoned, asking about Deane. She said she "just wanted to see him."

On the first anniversary of Deane's disappearance, Holden phoned all of them except Phillips and Sarah Atwood and invited them to a party at his store: a "survivors party," he called it. They all came, even Cherise from Oregon, and after they had a couple of drinks, they told Avery Deane stories.

"Few people besides Avery and Sandra have been able to find me in my little home in the woods," Cherise said." She spoke softly and tentatively, like someone not used to talking, and, instead of drinking beer or wine like the rest of them, she sipped from time to time from a small vial she carried in a pouch tied around her waist. "When I saw your car coming slowly down the dirt road, I was going to disappear," she explained to Sandra, "but I had a premonition that I should greet you." Disappear? Holden wondered about that. "Of course, Avery was not human, and I understood that from the first. He was a spirit, wrapped in lightning and energy. He couldn't be still.

"He asked me for six colors. They were the six colors of ancient Chinese culture, the ones they called the 'true colors': imperial yellow, gold, light blue, medium blue, deep blue and russet. I knew he was on an important quest and that I had been chosen to take a small part in it. I had never before been selected to do great things, but Avery called on me. I was surprised that he paid me the first time. Sprites are careless about money. They will say anything; do anything. It's all the same to them. A half-year later, still on his mission, he again asked for my help, and this time he didn't pay. Now he has passed on to wherever spirits go. We won't see him again, I think."

Holden would not have said that Cherise was smiling, but there was something like a smile playing on her face. She looked pleased with the roll she had played in the Avery Deane story. It suited her. She just added this, and then she was done talking for the evening: "People aren't made to make their way alone. We try to be true to our calling, whatever it is, and to do a good job. But we need something other, something outside of us, a spirit, a person, an audience, a reader to make us have meaning. That's what Avery is. He is a spirit who gave my work with color meaning. That was payment enough."

Holden looked around his showroom, caught as he had been so often by the beauty of the rugs that had somehow survived decades of being walked on, danced on, prayed on and preyed on and loved and ignored and stored and treasured and had wound up here on his walls, at least for a time.

"Well, I don't know about him being a 'spirit,'" Sandra broke the silence. "I suppose he was just another man, mainly. He still is. He's not dead, you know. He must be out there someplace." She seemed sad. "It's just that I had such a good time running around with him and finding you out in Oregon, Cherise, and going around to Holden's store and here and there.

"He loved the room he rented form me, the doily unit. I think all my tenants have liked the doilies, but Avery was the only one who ever said so. He could talk about each one of them. I helped him wind up the wool that you ladies spun." She smiled at the four friends from Little Kabul. "He paid me

231

rent for a while and then he didn't. Then he paid up again and then he beat me for three month's rent. I don't really care. I think he was broke or he would have paid me." She swirled her drink. "We ran around together for a while, but I knew he was never going to stay. As you said, Cherise, he couldn't stay still. So, I wish him well if he's alive, which I hope he is."

Clem told the other survivors that Deane had caused him a lot of trouble. "The son of a bitch nearly killed all the vines. That's all that place is is vines. Ninety years old. Then I had to come back and save them. Hell, I don't mind. The truth is, I had gotten tired of the old farm until that Brit or whatever he is came along. Then we drove around the farm and he thought it was swell. I got excited about it all over again. He's the kind of guy that can get you all wound up about something. Did me, anyway. That's worth something, isn't it? I don't know if the fellow was a crook or a saint. Or a spirit like you say. But I like working the vines again. I guess I'll just putter around out there until I pass on. No harm in that." Clem caught his breath after all his talking.

"He had some kind of voice, didn't he? Loudest son-of-a-bitch I ever did hear." He shook his head.

Zainab spoke for the spinners. "He was nice to us. He liked to watch us spin. He said we were magic." She laughed. "It's good that somebody liked what we do. He paid us for the first job."

Khalil took his turn. "Man, I don't know who he was or what he was. There's a lot about this country and the people that I never have understood, even if he didn't come from here. He made me promise not to talk about some things. That's okay. He was the boss. I think about it and I can't

232

understand how I could have given up a half of a year away from the restaurant to work on Avery's rugs. It was crazy. But he got me to do it. How did he get everyone to do all those things? He made everything a lot of fun, that's how.

"Sitting at the loom again after all those years got me to thinking again about Afghanistan. All my people in the North. I want to take my family back there for a while to meet my people. I don't know what they'll think of Star. They'll love her. But she'd better be a little more modest. They'll teach her.

"But Avery...what the heck was he, Holden? It seems like you knew him better than anyone. Was he a crook? Because some of the things he swore me to secrecy about may not be so good, if you know what I mean. Or was he a good guy, or what?"

Holden thought he had figured it out. Because, when he had opened that package, expecting to see either a silk Kirman or a worthless, worn-out rug, he had instead found something so strange that he could at first make no sense of it at all. There was the dragon, staring at him, the gold field and flaming pearls and wave-patterns. There was the Ferrier Dragon Rug: old, breathtaking, gorgeous, fleecy, alive. It was the rug he had seen on the wall of the museum just a week before, and now he held it in his own trembling hands there in his little behind-the-store apartment. He wanted to run to the street and stop Avery and say, "There's been a mistake..."

There was something different about it, though. He knew there was, but he couldn't see it. He counted the toes of the dragon. Five. That was the same. What was different? He couldn't place it, but suddenly he knew that it was not the same rug, not the Ferrier rug. Where there *two* Ferrier rugs? And what was Deane doing with one of them?

The truth, when he suddenly understood it, snapped his head back and shut his eyes. No, there was *no* Ferrier rug, or, if there was, it wasn't the rug he held, nor was it the rug in the museum. This rug, the second one, totally destroyed the validity of the first. Two of them turn up at the same time? Obviously made by the same weaver; in the same condition; the same patterns of wear? They were both fakes. Incredible, fantastic, impossible fakes—incredible, that is, that someone *could* fake them, that someone could make rugs that were so good. And who had made them? Avery Deane. That's what he had had Khalil weaving.

Holden opened his eyes now and admired the rug's undiminished beauty. How could he have done this? How could Avery have made something so good? And how could he have been so dishonest as to sell it, rug number one, as the Ferrier Dragon Rug? He had made and sold a fake, a forgery.

It occurred to Holden that this rug suddenly made Ulysses Pope's rug worthless. No, not worthless, but worth far less than the amount of money Avery had carried in his briefcase. Not only that, but it made a liar out of Marley Phillips, who had authenticated it. And he supposed that it also made a monkey out of Sarah Atwood who had been so obviously triumphant to land it for the museum. He smiled. "Is that why he gave it to me?" he wondered. "For me to revenge myself on those three? Or just to pay off his debts to me? Fake or not, this rug is worth far more than what he owed me. Or just for fun?" He didn't know. But he didn't seriously consider coming forward with this rug for revenge or for money. "A friend gave it to me," he thought. "I should keep it."

And so Holden carefully moth-proofed the rug and finally threw it down the black hole of Calcutta, to be pulled out and opened some distant day. And when he had tossed it down the shoot and still sat on his bed and thought about everything, he believed he now had the clue he needed to understand Avery Deane.

So when Khalil asked Holden who or what Avery Deane was, he answered, "He was an artist. Nothing else was important to him: not money, not love, not fame, not us. Oh, I think he liked a few people, but he used us for his ends, and his end was to make rugs. They were his medium. And the rugs he made were works of art.

"I used to wonder whether he was a con man." Holden laughed. "Maybe artists *are* con men. And maybe art is an illusion, if not a lie. That's what Avery used to say. I mean, those people up on the stage are just pretending, aren't they? They're *acting*, creating an illusion. And the plot of a novel isn't something that really happened, is it? It's just a story. That's why they call it fiction. The perspective in a painting is nothing more than a tricky way of making a one-dimensional medium seem like three. And that portrait of George Washington—it's not Washington. It's an impression, an illusion, a series of tricks." Holden could have gone on, but what he was thinking about were Avery's rug's. Now *there* was illusion: making something brand new look nearly 400 years old.

"Anyway," Holden went on, "that was the fire in Avery's belly: his rugs, his art. That was his right and wrong. That was his testosterone. It was his reason to borrow and lie and finagle. Or at least that's what I think."

The others didn't know whether they understood what Holden had just said. Cherise still thought Avery was a spirit.

Holden laughed out loud. Actually, everyone was having a good time and doing a fair amount of laughing. But Holden laughed because suddenly now, a year after he had thrown the dragon rug down the black hole, it came to him how the rug Deane had given him was different from the rug that had become the official Ferrier Dragon Rug. Just like the rug Pope had bought, his rug's dragon stared and glowered and maybe even accused: "Who are you," it seemed to ask. But this dragon's stare could only get so intense and only so accusatory. Just one of its eyes was open. The other was closed in what could only be a wink.

2640190

Made in the USA